Home A

Games
for the Commodore 64

by

Timothy P. Banse

Home Applications and Games for the Commodore 64
2019 Edition
by Timothy P. Banse

Library of Congress Cataloging in Publication Data

Banse, Timothy P.
Home applications and games for the Commodore 64.
1. Commodore 64 (Computer)—Programming.
2. Basic (Computer program language) 3. Computer
programs. I. Title. II. Series.
QA76.8.C64B35 1985 005.325 84-23360
ISBN: 978 0 934523 90 5

Library of Congress Catalog Card Number 84-23360

Editor @Middle-Coast-Publishing.com

Good Books Are Where We Find Our Dreams

MIDDLE
COAST
PUBLISHING

Iowa City, Iowa

HOW TO USE THIS BOOK

```
**** CBM BASIC V2 ****
3583 BYTES FREE
READY.
```

   This book provides a set of ready-to-run programs for use with your Commodore 64. Each program comes with background information on the topic of the chapter, an explanation of how each program works and a variable table that lists what each variable stands for. So it's possible either to jump into the book and simply type in and run a program, or in the alternative, to approach each chapter as a learning experience.

How To Save Time Typing in Programs

   When you type in the programs, you'll notice some are fairly long. Don't be discouraged. Consider omitting REM statements because doing so shortens the time spent typing them in. JUST DON'T MESS UP THE PROGRAM NUMBERS!
   Another trick for reducing the tedium of typing is to replace every PRINT command with the question mark **?**. For example, typing in 100 **?** "This" creates the same effect as: 100 PRINT "This", but takes four fewer keystrokes. Using the "**?**" abbreviation can save a great deal of programming time and agony. Even more salient, the shorter a program, the faster it runs!

How To Personalize the Programs

This book was written to be used by anyone owning a Commodore 64 and datassete recorder. You don't need a printer except for Chapter 11, and, with the exception of Chapter 31, you don't need a disk drive. But what if you do own one of these peripherals? No problem; simply customize the programs to take advantage of all that fancy gear. Here's how. If you own a printer, you may want to insert the following program lines wherever you want the appropriate information displayed on the screen.

```
695 REM *** USE PRINTER ***
696 OPEN 3,4
765 REM ** PRINT OUT ***
766 PRINT #3, CHR$(BY);
```

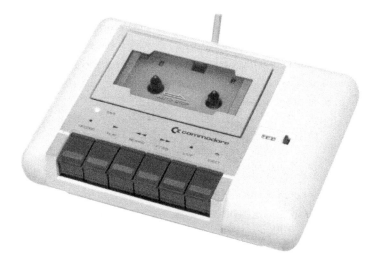

In this case, we've modified the Crypto System program in Chapter 6 to make a printout of the decrypted cassette file. Another option would be to funnel everything that's normally displayed on the screen to the printer, instead of just a few selected items. Let's modify the Checkbook program

(Chapter 1) to show you how.

```
95 REM *** USE PRINTER ***
96 OPEN 3,4
97 REM *** DIVERT SCREEN DISPLAY TO PRINTER ***
98 CMD 3
```

From now on, everything that's normally displayed on the TV shows up on the printer paper, including "READY". Please note that in the case of the Checkbook program, since the color of the border can't be changed to red when a check bounces, you'll have to rely on the blunder sound to catch your attention.

If you own a disk drive, it's very easy to modify the cassette programs. Wherever a program opens a cassette file for a read with the command:

```
OPEN 1,1,0,
```

Simply replace it with the diskette command:

```
OPEN 1,8,2, "0:FILENAME,SEQ,READ"
```

Whenever the program writes information to the cassette tape, change the OPEN 1,1,2 to read:

```
OPEN 1,8,3, "0:FILENAME,SEQ,WRITE".
```

In both cases where we changed to diskette commands, the zero immediately following the quotation marks stands for disk drive zero, FILENAME should be replaced by a filename of your choosing, and SEQ tells the Commodore 64 we're writing to a sequential file.

Finally, if you'd rather forego the labor of typing in these programs, you don't have too. Middle Coast Publishing has made available a USB thumb drive with all 32 programs stored in memory. The package also includes program updates and modifications.

Middle Coast Publishing
P.O. Box 535
Hills, IA 52235-0535.

2019 Update for C64 and C64 Mini

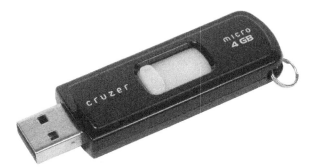

*When a FAT 32 formatted USB memory stick is plugged into Retro Games C64, **before** BASIC is launched, BASIC code can be saved to the memory stick.*

Saving and Loading On The C64 Mini

There are two available methods for saving BASIC programs:

1. Press the MENU button and select 'Save/Load game' and then save to an available slot on THEC64 Mini as you would do for a game. In the User Guide PDF, see: CHAPTER 5: PLAYING GAMES for more details on saving and loading to slots.
2. If a compatible USB memory stick (formatted to FAT32) is attached to THEC64 Mini before BASIC is launched, then you can save your BASIC code to the memory stick. When launching BASIC, THEC64 Mini looks for a specific disk image file on the memory stick. If the file isn't found, then a THEC64-drive8.d64 file is automatically created on the USB memory stick for you. You will then be able to save and load to and from this file from BASIC.

Please note that in order to accommodate both THEC64 Joystick, a USB Keyboard and a USB memory stick at the same time, you need to connect a separate USB hub (not included) to gain additional USB ports. Know that Retro Games Ltd does guarantee that all USB hubs will work with THEC64 Mini and some hubs require a separate power source.

SAVE

With a compatible USB memory stick connected, you can save to the disk image using the standard SAVE to disk command:

```
SAVE "RGL",8
```

The name of the file goes between the quotation marks and can be whatever you like, so long as it it's no longer than 15 characters. In this example, it's just three, nice and short (RGL). The number 8 after the filename is a device ID number that is allocated to the disk image file on your USB memory stick

Press RETURN afterwards to begin the save

BASIC will report SAVING followed by your chosen filename, and when it is completed, it returns to the READY prompt and the square cursor

To save over an existing file with the same filename, add **@0** to the front, like this:

```
SAVE @0:RGL",8
```

Please be aware that C64 BASIC won't give any warnings that you are overwriting a file when you do this.

VERIFY

You can check that the save worked by using the VERIFY keyword, thusly:

```
VERIFY "RGL",8
```

If all is well, you will see:

```
VERIFYING
```

followed by:

```
OK
READY
```

How To LOAD a Saved Program

Once more ensure that the same USB storage device is connected to THEC64 Mini before you run BASIC, and then type the following command in BASIC to get your program back.

```
LOAD "RGL",8
```

How To See What's Stored on the Disk

From BASIC, you can look at a disk and see what files are on there. To do that requires use of the LOAD command, but in a slightly different way from before. Instead of typing a filename we are using the reserved variable $.

```
LOAD "$",8
```

BASIC will report SEARCHING FOR $ followed by LOADING and then return to the READY prompt once again.

To see what's on the disk, simply type the following command:

```
LIST
```

Instead of listing BASIC code, this time the command displays what's stored on the disk.

In the above example, we have just one program on the disk and it's the program just saved named RGL. The program uses 1 block on the disk with 63 blocks remaining free to save programs at a future date.

Be aware that if you load the directory of a disk and have some BASIC code on the C64 at the same time, the $ listing will replace the BASIC listing in the computer's memory and you will lose your program, if you haven't already saved it.

If you want to use multiple disks, then you will need to use a different USB memory stick for each disk, or temporarily rename the files because the .D64 file is always saved with the same filename:

```
THEC64-drive8.d64
```

each time.

Read Only

If you don't have a USB storage device plugged into the port, but decide to try saving to device 8 anyway, BASIC will appear like it has successfully saved but when you load the directory of the disk it will be empty. This is because without USB storage, BASIC uses a disk image that can only be read, not saved to. The teltale sign is the name of the disk, which is READONLY instead of THEC64. The disk is completely empty and cannot have anything saved to it

To overcome this, you can always save in one of the four save slots, switch off THEC64, insert a USB memory stick into a spare USB port, switch THEC64 Mini back on, load BASIC, restore the save slot and then save to the D64 disk image using the SAVE command detailed earlier. Device 8 will now be the disk image on the USB memory stick

CONTENTS

Checkbook Balancer

No doubt you've seen those fancy checkbook balancers designed to run on your micro. They keep the balance up to date, the number of each check, tell who was paid and on what date. The problem is, it takes longer to run the program than to simply figure it out in your head and write down the results with a ballpoint pen. Want to keep things simple? Here's a quick and easy way to keep the balance up to date. It's fast and accurate.

A checkbook balancer is a handy tool. With one, it takes very little work to keep the balance up to date, allowing you always to know exactly how much money you have in your bank account. First, enter the current balance. Then, one at a time, enter the amount of each check you've written. If the balance drops below zero—forbidden by the bank—an overdrawn message will flash on the screen, and the border will turn red. The amount overdrawn will be displayed as the balance. If you need to find out the extent of the damages, keep entering the other checks and keep an eye on the total overdraft figure.

On the other hand, if the balance remains in the black, as each check is entered, it will be subtracted from the old balance, and the new amount will be tallied and printed on the screen. When the figuring is finished, pencil the new balance in the checkbook. If you want to add a deposit to the account, simply hit the space bar when asked for the check's amount. Then enter the amount of the deposit.

Here's another use for the program. Use it as a budgeting tool to keep track of cash flow. At the end of the month, go through the checkbook and enter just the checks written to a particular category, say, the grocery. When totaled, you'll know if you are exceeding the amount of dollars allocated for food, for entertainment, and so on.

For this application, instead o entering the true balance of the account at the start of the program, enter the amount budgeted for that category.

If you go over the amount, the overdrawn message will flash on the screen and the display will tell you how far over the limit you may have wandered.

How the Program Works

Line 80 blanks the screen.
Line 90 assigns the variable BA the value of zero.
Line 110 specifies black characters. Line 120 displays CHECKBOOK BALANCER in black characters.
Line 170 asks for the current balance. Using a semicolon and a colon after a PRINT statement and before an INPUT prints the prompt (?) on the same line as the print statement.
Line 220 asks for the amount of the next check.
Line 240 looks for a carriage return, the signal you want to make a deposit. If so, go to line 500.
Line 260 converts the string variable with the check's amount stored in it to a numeric dollar amount.
Line 280 subtracts the latest check from the balance.
Line 300 checks the balance. If no money is left in the account, go to the subroutine at line 420.
Line 340 specifies white characters.
Line 350 displays the balance in white characters.
Line 360 empties CH$.
Line 370 branches the program to line 180 for next entry.
Line 420 turns the screen border red.
Line 450 displays OVERDRAWN.
Lines 500 through 530 add money to the account.

String and Numeric Variables

BA Tells how much money left in account.
CH$ Check amount.

REM = ?

CH Dollar amount of last check written.
DO Amount of deposit.

The Program

```
10  REM ********************
20  REM *
30  REM *
40  REM * CHECKBOOK BALANCER *
50  REM *
60  REM *
70  REM *********************
80  PRINT CHR$(147)
90  BA = 0
100 REM *** BLACK CHARS. ***
110 PRINT CHR$(144)
120 PRINT SPC(2) "CHECKBOOK BALANCER"
130 PRINT
140 REM *** WHITE CHARACTERS ***
150 PRINT CHR$(5)
160 REM *** GET BALANCE ***
170 PRINT "BALANCE";:INPUT BA
180 PRINT
190 REM *** BLACK CHARS. ***
200 PRINT CHR$(144)
210 REM *** CHECK'S AMOUNT ***
220 PRINT "AMOUNT";:INPUT CH$
230 REM *** WANT TO ADD DEPOSIT ***
240 IF CH$ = "" THEN 500
250 REM *** CONVERT VARIABLE TO NUMERIC ***
260 LET CH=VAL (CH$)
270 REM *** FIGURE NEW BALANCE ***
280 BA = BA - CH
290 REM *** SEE IF ACOUNT OVERDRAWN ***
```

3

```
300 IF BA < 0 THEN GOSUB 420
310 PRINT
320 IF BA > 0 THEN POKE 53280,6
330 REM *** WHITE CHARACTERS ***
340 PRINT CHR$(5)
350 PRINT "BALANCE ";BA
360 CH$ = ""
370 GOTO 180
380 REM ********************
390 REM *OVERDRAWN*
400 REM
410 REM *** RED BORDER ***
420 POKE 53280,2
430 REM *** RED CHARS. ***
440 PRINT CHR$(28)
450 PRINT "OVERDRAWN"
460 RETURN
470 REM ***********************
480 REM *** RECORD A DEPOSIT ***
490 REM ***********************
500 PRINT
510 PRINT "DEPOSIT ";:INPUT DO
520 BA = BA + DO
530 GOTO 310
READY
```

Budget Power

A budget is a simple concept. How much do the bills total during the budget period, and how much money is available to pay those liabilities? The budget power program lets you plug in those cash flow variables and make plans according to the results. Expenses are categorized in the way they are encountered by the average house-hold, but it is easy to switch the categories you don't need for ones you do.

RUN the program and fill in how many dollars you have to cover the budget period. Fill in each budget item amount. Once these itemized expenses are totaled, a printout tells how much you need.

A budget can be manipulated as a creative tool. It need not be as rigid as the Federal government's. Figure yours a couple of different ways. Cut back on food and pay more on old loans with high interest rates. Consider the short- and long-term impact of your planning.

How the Program Works

Line 170 blanks the screen.
Line 190 prints the program title: BUDGET.
Line 230 asks how much money is available for the budget period.
Line 260 asks how much is needed for shelter during that same budget period.
Likewise, lines 280, 300, 320, 340 and so on, ask for the appropriate sums to handle each category of expense.
Line 560 tallies each amount and stores the result in the variable TA.
Line 590 prints the TA.

String and Numeric Variables

DL Dollars available to finance the budget period.
SH Projected amount needed to cover shelter expenses.
FD Projected amount needed to cover food expenses.
EL Projected amount needed to cover electricity and utility expenses.

TL Projected amount needed to cover telephone expenses.

CR Projected amount needed to cover car expenses.

LN Projected amount needed to cover loan expenses.

FL Projected amount needed to cover fuel expenses.

MI Projected amount needed to cover tire expenses.

IN Projected amount needed to cover insurance expenses.

LI Projected amount needed to cover life insurance expenses.

ME Projected amount needed to cover medical expenses.

CL Projected amount needed to cover clothes expenses.

EN Projected amount needed to cover entertainment expenses.

GA Projected amount needed to cover gambling expenses.

SL Projected amount needed to cover miscellaneous expenses.

TA The sum of money needed, based on the total of each of the categories, to meet the budget period's deficits.

The Program

```
100 REM ********************
110 REM *
120 REM *
130 REM * HOME BUDGET *
140 REM *
150 REM *
160 REM ********************
170 PRINT CHR$(147): REM *** BLANK THE SCREEN ***
180 PRINT
190 PRINT SPC(8) "BUDGET"
200 PRINT " -------------------- "
210 REM *** TOTAL AVAILABLE FOR BUDGET PERIOD ***
230 PRINT "HAVE $";:INPUT DL
240 REM *** AMOUNT NEEDED FOR EACH CATEGORY ***
250 PRINT
260 PRINT"RENT/MORTGATE";:INPUT SH
270 PRINT
280 PRINT "FOOD";:INPUT FD
290 PRINT
300 PRINT "UTILITIES";:INPUT EL
310 PRINT
```

```
320 PRINT "TELEPHONE";:INPUT TL
330 PRINT
340 PRINT "LOAN (CAR) ";:INPUT CR
350 PRINT
360 PRINT "INSTALLMENT";:INPUT LN
370 PRINT
380 PRINT "GAS/DIESEL FUEL";:INPUT FL
390 PRINT
400 PRINT "MISC. CAR";:INPUT MI
410 PRINT
420 PRINT "INSURANCE (CAR)";:INPUT IN
430 PRINT
440 PRINT "LIFE";:INPUT LE
450 PRINT
460 PRINT "DENTAL/MEDICAL";:INPUT ME
470 PRINT
480 PRINT "KIDS CLOTHES";:INPUT CL
490 PRINT
500 PRINT "ENTERTAINMENT";:INPUT EN
510 PRINT
520 PRINT " SAVINGS/INVEST";:INPUT GA
530 PRINT
540 PRINT "MISC. EXPENSE";: INPUT SL
550 REM *** SUM OF ALL THE BUDGET CATEGORIES ***
560 TA=SH+FD+EL+TL+CR+LN+FL+MI+IN+LI+ME+CL+EN+GA
570 REM *** DISPLAY THE AMOUNT NEEDED ***
580 PRINT "----------------------------------- "
590 PRINT "NEED $";TA
600 END
READY
```

3.
Number Averaging

It often seems our world is made up of numbers. This can be good because numbers help us keep track of our favorite players' batting averages or yards rushing, as well as our grades at school. This program makes it simple to figure the average for any kind of data.

Just enter each number, one at a time. Each entry can be up to 97 places long. After the last of the numbers is entered, and you see the next question mark prompt, hit RETURN. The numbers will be tallied and then displayed on the screen.

Here's what a sample run looks like:

```
? 1
? 2
? 47
? 10
? 5
? (carriage return)
TOTAL = 65
AVERAGE = 13
```

How the Program Works

Line 170 blanks the screen.
Line 180 dimensions the string variable NUMBER$. DIM (97) reserves space for a number up to 97 places long!
Line 250 inputs each number, one at a time, as a string variable.
Line 270 keeps track of how many numbers are entered.
Line 290 looks for a carriage return. If it finds one, the program quits taking numbers and averages the ones already entered.
Line 310 Remember we're inputting the numbers as string variables (NU$). Since we perform mathematical functions on them, we convert string variables to numeric with NU = VAL (NU$). The string variable "47" becomes the number 47.

8

Line 330 adds each new number to the total.

Line 350 empties NU$, then sends us back for each new number.

Line 400 is the beginning of the end. If line 290 found a carriage return, we subtract one from the number of entries, eliminating the carriage return as an entry.

Line 420 does the calculating.

Lines 440 through 470 print the sum of the numbers entered and their average.

String and Numeric Variables

NU$ Used to hold individual numbers that will be averaged.

CO Tells how many numbers have been entered for averaging.

NU Holds each number as a string variable.

(NU$) Once converted to a numeric, NU holds its value.

TA Is the sum of all the numbers entered.

AV The sum total (TA) divided by CO.

The Program

```
100 REM **************************
110 REM *
120 REM *
130 REM * NUMBER AVERAGING *
140 REM *
150 REM *
160 REM **************************
170 PRINT CHR$(147)
180 DIM NU$(97)
190 PRINT
200 PRINT SPC(3) "NUMBER AVERAGING"
210 PRINT:PRINT:PRINT
220 PRINT "WHICH NUMBERS:"
230 PRINT
240 REM *** ENTER EACH NUMBER ***
250 INPUT NU$
260 REM *** KEEP COUNT HOW MANY TO AVERAGE ***
270 CO=CO+1
```

```
280 REM ***-HIT RETURN TO TALLY***
290 IF NU$ = "" THEN 400
300 REM ***C0NVERT STRING VARIABLE TO NUMERIC ***
310 NU=VAL(NU$)
320 REM *** ADD NEW VALUE TOTAL***
330 TA=TA+ NU
340 REM *** GET ANOTHER NUMBER ***
350 NU$="":GOTO 250
360 REM ***********************
370 REM * READY TO AVERAGE *
380 REM *********************
390 REM *** DISCOUNT CARRIAGE RETURN ***
400 CO=CO - 1
410 REM *** DIVIDE TOTAL BY NUMBER OF ENTRIES ***
420 AV=TA/CO
430 REM *** DISPLAY RESULTS ***
440 PRINT
450 PRINT "TOTAL.=";TA
460 PRINT
470 PRINT "AVERAGE=";AV
480 END
```

4

Calorie Counter

Want a trimmer waistline? The best way to accomplish this would be to reduce food intake while increasing exercise. You don't have to become a world-class athlete. But if you like swimming, or walking in the park, or Aikido, or any other form of physical activity, it can help you lose weight.

There will be other benefits, of course, including enjoying better health and feeling better about how you look. You'll have more resistance to winter colds and flu. You'll sleep more soundly and enjoy better dreams. Besides all this, an exercise program will give you a magnificent opportunity to meet new people with similar interests. Perhaps the biggest plus will be your new-found control over your appetite. You'll be a lean jungle cat running on the edge of hungry.

Although the best plan to lose weight would include both diet and exercise, what if you truly want to lose weight but love to eat? The idea of actually cutting back on meals may be frightening. If so, there is still an answer in exercise.

Say you don't eat any more, or any less. But you do add an evening walk around the city park. Just by taking that little stroll daily, and doing nothing else, you could lose fourteen pounds in one year.

Now to the program. This diet helper asks how much you weigh, how much you want to weigh, and how many days you want to take to reach the target weight. After you fill in your vital information, the TV screen will display the total number of calories you'll need to burn off. Don't be dismayed. Even a couple of pounds seems to equal an astronomical number of calories.

The computer takes those calories, matches them up with the number of days until the target weight will be reached, and spells out how many calories per day you'll need to cut back to reach your goal.

ACTIVITY	CALORIES BURNED
Bicycling 6 mph	240
Bicycling 12 mph	410
Cross-country skiing	700
Jogging 6 mph	660
Jogging 7 mph	920
Jumping rope	750
Running 10 mph	1280
Swimming	275 to 500
Tennis	400
Walking 2 mph	240
Walking 3 mph	320
Walking 4 mph	440

Average Calories Burned Per Hour by a 150-Pound Person.

For a 100-pound person, reduce number of calories burned by 30-percent.

For a 200-pound person, multiply by 1.3.

Know that exercising harder, or faster, per given activity, barely increases the number of calories burned. To burn up a larger amount of calories, exercise for a longer period of time.

Take those calories, mix diet and exercise to lose them, and soon you'll weigh in at fighting trim. One word of caution. Don't be in too big of a hurry to lose all the weight all at once. Two pounds or so a week is a sensible loss. Conduct a Spartan boot camp for yourself, and discouragement is likely to set in. Take it easy on yourself and enjoy life: Fit, trim, and healthy.

How the Program Works

Line 170 blanks the screen.

Line 190 displays the program title.

Line 220 inputs the variable CU, current weight.

Line 250 inputs the variable DE, desired weight.

Line 270 inputs the variable DY, days until goal.

Line 290 calculates how many pounds you want to lose.

Line 310 converts pounds to calories.

Lines 330 through 350 calculate how many calories need to be burned up a day in order to lose the weight during the specified period of time.

Lines 360 through 420 display the results.

String and Numeric Variables

CU Tells the computer how much you weigh.

DE Tells the computer how much you ought to weigh.

DY Tells how long you're allowing to remove those extra pounds.

LO Result of subtracting how much you want to weigh from what you weigh.

CA How many calories you need to burn up.

DL How many calories you need to burn up each day.

The Program

```
100 REM *
110 REM *
120 REM *
130 REM * WEIGHT LOSS TALLY *
140 REM *
150 REM *
160 REM *
170 PRINT CHR$(147):REM *** BLANK THE SCREEN ***
180 PRINT
190 PRINT SPC(4) "WEIGHT WATCHER"
200 PRINT:PRINT
210 REM *** TODAY'S WEIGHT ***
220 PRINT "WEIGHT";:INPUT CU
230 PRINT:PRINT
240 REM *** DESIRED WEIGHT ***
250 PRINT "DESIRED WEIGHT";:INPUT DE
260 PRINT:PRINT
270 PRINT "DAYS UNTIL GOAL";:INPUT DY
280 REM *** WEIGHT LOSS GOAL. ***
290 LO=CU-DE
300 REM *** CONVERT POUNDS TO CALORIES ***
310 CA=LO*3500
320 REM *** FIGURE DAILY CALORIE LOSS ***
330 DL=CA/DY
340 REM *** CONVERT TO TWO PLACE DECIMAL ***
350 DL=INT (DL + . 5)
360 PRINT:PRINT
370 REM *** DISPLAY PROGRAM RESULTS ***
380 PRINT "CALORIES TO LOSE:"
390 PRINT:PRINT
400 PRINT "TOTAL";CA
410 PRINT:PRINT
420 PRINT "PER DAY";DL
430 END
READY.
```

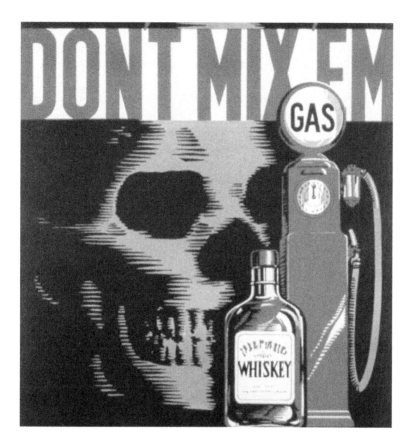

5

Blood Alcohol Test

This program can give you an idea of where you stand, or wobble, legally. If you're planning an evening of social drinking, keep in mind that drunk driving laws are getting tougher. To find out if you will be bending the law, first plug in your vital statistics and see if you pass. If you go over the legal limit, then the program will display a message telling you so.

It's true the capacity for alcohol varies from person to person. How well we maintain ourselves depends on our weight, body chemistry, and how fast, and what we drink. Also important is whether our stomach is full or empty.

First, RUN the program, then enter your weight and how many ounces of alcohol you've imbibed. Next, enter the proof of the drink. This, by the way, is the only complicated part of the procedure.

Straight whiskey, for example, might be labeled 86 or 100 proof. Proof is twice the alcoholic percentage. Therefore, 3.2 beer is 6.4 proof, 12 percent wine is 24 proof, and a highball, even though made up of a 100-proof vodka, won't be a 100-proof drink. If it's a nine-ounce drink, mixed with one-ounce of vodka and eight-ounces of orange juice, it's about 12 proof. That information should help in computing the actual proof of what you're drinking.

The result of all this computation will represent the approximate blood/alcohol level in your bloodstream. Each state has a specific blood/alcohol level that determines whether or not you are legally drunk. Line 340 in the program uses .1 (percent) as the legal limit. If you don't know your state's legal limit, a phone call to the state police will get you the answer.

How the Program Works

Line 170 blanks the screen.
Line 210 inputs your weight in pounds.
Line 230 inputs ounces of; the drink.
Line 250 inputs the actual proof of the beverage.
Line 290 calculates the percentage of alcohol in your bloodstream and converts the percentage into a two-place decimal.
Line 320 prints the blood/alcohol level.
Line 340 checks to see whether or not you are legally drunk; if so, then prints LEGALLY DRUNK.

String and Numeric Variables

WE Supplies the drunk/sober formula with your body weight in pounds.
OU Ounces imbibed.
PR. Actual proof of drink, mixed or straight.
PE How much alcohol is in your bloodstream.

The Program

```
100 REM ******************
110 REM *
120 REM *
130 REM * BLOOD ALCOHOL *
140 REM *
150 REM * *
160 REM ******************
170 PRINT CHR$(147):REM CLEAR SCREEN
180 PRINT
190 PRINT SPC(1) "BLOOD ALCOHOL LEVEL"
200 PRINT:PRINT '
210 PRINT "YOUR WEIGHT";:INPUT WE
220 PRINT:PRINT
230 PRINT "OUNCES ALCOHOL";:INPUT OU
240 PRINT:PRINT
250 PRINT "PROOF";:INPUT PR
260 REM * CALCULATE PERCENTAGE OF ALCOHOL IN BLOOD *
270 PE = (OU * PR * .037) /WE)
280 REM *** CONVERT TO TWO PLACE DECIMAL ***
290 FE=INT(((PE * 100) + 0.5) / 100
300 REM *** DISPLAY RESULTS ***
310 PRINT:PRINT
320 PRINT "BLOOD LEVEL = ";PE
330 REM *** IF DRUNK DISPLAY WARNING ***
340 IF PE > .10 THEN PRINT:PRINT"LEGALLY DRUNK"
350 END
READY
```

6.

Secrets
for
Sale . . .

The Commodore 64 Crypto System

Most crypto systems create lines of text, broken down into five-character mystery words, that look exactly like what they are: Garbled text. The scenario looks suspicious at first sight. There's little doubt that there's a secret lurking in those cipher text shadows, a dark secret the owner doesn't want you to know. For microcomputer whiz kids and business spooks, it creates an instant challenge.

The beauty and truth of this crypto scheme is that it creates something quite unlike other crypto systems. If someone stumbles across a sacred file, all that's seen is a cassette tape labeled: Light & Sound Show Driver. But what happens if they LOAD the program and try to RUN?

Simple.

The program runs, giving them a very pleasing spectacle of what kinds of colors, bells, and whistles the Commodore 64 computer can conjure up. Nothing mysterious here. And better yet, since it doesn't look like a secret code, no one tries to decipher the message.

Know that hiding secrets goes back to the olden days, to ancient Greece, in fact, where slaves' heads were shaved and secret messages tattooed on their scalps.

18

Once the hair bristles were sufficient to hide the tattooed secrets, the slaves were dispatched to their destinies at the battle front. The technique of concealing messages is called steganography.

Cryptography is another science handed down from ancient Greece. Crypto means hidden and graphy means writing. Therefore, cryptography is the science of secret writing, the purpose of which is to prevent or delay an enemy or unauthorized person from obtaining intelligence by reading intercepted communications. Whew! In the lingo of the eighties, that means enforcing your right to privacy.

To put both secret crafts into practice, first write the message in plain text, then read it back. Does it say exactly what you want it to say, in as few words as possible? Use abbreviations whenever possible, but only when the meaning is unmistakable. Use single words in place of whole sentences. Minimize the use of articles such as a, an, and the.` In secret message writing, do not use punctuation. Do not use the expression S-T-O-P. Instead, use the following abbreviations: ques for question mark, paren for a parenthetical expression, pd for period, cmm for comma, and quote/unquote instead of quotation marks. Do not repeat. Repetition leads to broken code. Furthermore, numbers should be spelled out, i.e., seven, nine, three.

With the clear text message ready for encryption, RUN the program. It will ask for a code word. The standard admonitions apply in choosing a code word for encryption or time-sharing: Don't use your name, your lover's name, street address, or anything obvious. Don't make it easy for a spy to compromise your secrets. Password entered, the computer will do a simple cipher substitution encryption, translating your clear text into cipher text file.

That cassette file's scrambled text can be read and decrypted, but only if you know the password. A stranger using a READ program will simply see a strange mix of graphics characters. For security reasons, it helps to disguise the encrypted message by labeling the cassette tape as: DATA FOR LIGHT & SOUND SHOW.

The light and sound show program will read the tape and use it to drive a flashy show. That way, if anyone loads the tape into memory and runs it, a light and sound show will provide delight for hours or until some other intrigue intervenes.

How the Program Works (Encrypt)

Line 170 dimensions the variables we'll be relying on for character transposition.
Lines 190 through 240 display the menu and get that choice.
Line 270 asks for a code word to be used in the encryption process.
Line 280 converts the code word into a code number.
Lines 290 through 350 display the encryption instructions.

Line 370 opens the cassette channel to receive encrypted data.

Line 380 blanks the screen.

Line 390 prompts the user to enter a clear text line.

Line 410 takes a single character, a word, or a sentence, up to a maximum of 80 characters in length.

Line 420 looks for a carriage return. If the user enters a carriage return without any preceding text, it's the signal to quit encrypting.

Lines 440 through 510 do the encrypting.

Line 460 will take each character in SE$ and convert it to its ASCII number. The ASCII number is simply a number the computer understands. For instance, it thinks of the letter A as the number 65.

Line 480 The ASCII number is added to the code word's ASCII number to disguise it.

Line 500 adds each character to the string variable LI$. In essence, LI$ is SE$ encrypted.

Line 530 sends LI$ to the cassette file as encrypted text.

Line 420 looks for a carriage return. When one is found, we go to line 560 where the cassette file is closed.

Line 510 branches back for the next SE$ to be encrypted.

How the Decryption Program Works

Line 590 blanks the screen.

Line 600 asks for the code word used to encrypt the message.

Line 620 blanks the screen.

Lines 630 through 680 print decryption instructions.

Line 690 blanks the screen.

Line 700 opens the cassette channel for a read.

Line 710 reads characters from the cassette file, one by one.

Line 740 de-crypts BY.

Line 760 converts the decrypted character to its string variable equivalent and then prints it. Remember, we said the computer thought of the letter "A" as the number 65. Well, if the decrypted BY was 65, line 760 would display an "A".

Line 770 sends us back for the next character as long as we haven't read to the end of the file. Once we find the end of the cassette file, line 790 closes it.

String and Numeric Variables

CD$ The code word used in the encryption formula.

CD The ASCII number for code word.

SE$ The clear text character, word, or sentence to be encrypted.
LI$ Is variable SE$ encrypted.
BY$ The individual string variable from SE$.
BY Holds the ASCII number for BY$.
KE$ Any key pressed?

The Program

```
100 REM **********************
110 REM * *
120 REM * *
130 REM * CRYPTO SYSTEM *
140 REM * *
150 REM * *
160 REM **********************
170 DIM CD$(80), LI$(80), SE$ (80)
180 PRINT CHR$(147)
190 PRINT SPC(4) "CRYPTO SYSTEM"
200 PRINT
210 PRINT "1. ENCRYPT"
220 PRINT
230 PRINT "2. DECRYPT"
240 GET KE$= IF KE$ = "" THEN 240
250 KE = ASC(KE$)
260 ON KE - 48 GOTO 270,590
270 PRINT:PRINT "CODE WORD";:INPUT CD$
280 CD = ASC(CD$)
290 PRINT:PRINT SPC(2) "ABOUT TO ENCRYPT"
300 PRINT
310 PRINT:PRINT "1. INSERT BLANK TAPE"
320 PRINT:PRINT "2. COUNTER TO ZERO"
330 PRINT:PRINT "3. PRESS RECORD/PLAY"
340 PRINT:PRINT "4. HIT RETURN"
350 PRINT:PRINT "5. WAIT FOR PROMPT"
360 REM *** WRITE TO CASSETTE ***
370 OPEN 1,1,2
380 PRINT CHR$(147)
390 PRINT SPC(2⟩ "WORDS TO ENCRYFT"
400 PRINT
410 INPUT SE$
```

```
420 IF SE$= "" THEN GOTO 560
450 REM *** LENGTH OF LINE ***
440 FOR X= 1 TO LEN(SE$)
450 REM *** TAKE APART LETTER BY LETTER ***
460 BY$ = MID$ (SE,X,1)
470 REM *** ENCRYPT LETTER BY LETTER ***
480 LET BY = ASC(BY$) + CD
490 LET BY$=CHR$(BY)
500 LI$=LI$+BY$
510 NEXT X
520 REM *** WRITE LINE TO CASSETTE ***
530 PRINT#1,LI$
540 LI$ = "" : SE$ = ""
550 GOTO 410
560 CLOSE 1
570 REM *** RETURN TO MENU ***
580 GOTO 180
590 PRINT CHR$(147)
600 PRINT "CODE WORD";:INPUT CD$
610 CD = ASC(CD$)
620 PRINT CHR$(147)
630 PRINT SPC(3) "ABOUT TO DECRYPT"
640 PRINT
650 PRINT:PRINT "1. REWIND TAPE"
660 PRINT:PRINT "2. COUNTER TO ZERO"
670 PRINT:PRINT "5. PRESS PLAY BUTTON"
680 PRINT:PRINT "4. HIT RETURN"
685 PRINT CHR$(147)
690 OPEN 1,1,0
700 REM *** READ TAPE ***
710 GET #1, BY$
720 REM *** DECRYPT CHARACTER BY CHARACTER ***
730 BY=ASC(BY$)
740 BY = BY -CD
750 IF BY < 0 THEN PRINT: GOTO 770
760 PRINT CHR$(BY);
770 IF ST <> 64 THEN 710
780 PRINT
790 CLOSE 1
800 GET KE$:IF KE$ = "" THEN 800
```

```
810 CLR
880 GOTO 180
```

Light and Sound Show

The light show flashes a cloak of many colors on the screen, thanks to Commodore 64 graphics, accompanied by its very own ballad. While the show is meant to be driven by data generated by the crypto program, it's perfectly feasible to write your own set of values. However, only programmers with graphics experience will find this easy. If you're game, choose the musical notes you wish played and intersperse them with alternating border colors.

How the Program Works

Line 180 blanks the screen.

Line 240 Opens the cassette channel for a read. Line 310 reads the first four bytes and stores them in string variables.

Line 350 checks to see whether or not we've read to the end of the file. If not, then read some more values to plug into the light and sound show. If we have read to the end of the file, then close the channel and end the program.

Lines 360 through 390 convert those string variables into numbers,numbers we can plug into the Commodore 64 to create sound and color.

Line 430 plugs two of those numbers into the memory location that controls the screen and border's color.

Lines 470 through 500 plug numbers into the sound registers.

Line 550's loop holds the musical note for a beat, determined by a random number.

Line 570 closes the "Driver File", once we've read to the end.

Line 580 restores the screen to its normal colors.

String and Numeric Variables

AA$/AA First musical note.

BB$/BB Second musical note.

CC$/CC Third musical note.

DD$/DD Border color.

DE Delay loop plays tone for a random count.

ST Commodore 64 system variable. Flags end of a file.

```
100 REM ***********************
110 REM * *
120 REM * *
130 REM * LIGHT & SOUND *
140 REM * *
150 REM * EXTRAVAGANZA *
160 REM * *
170 REM ************************
180 PRINT CHR$(147)
190 PRINT
200 PRINT SPC(10) "PLEASE WAIT"
210 REM ****************
220 REM *** OPEN TAPE ***
230 REM ****************
240 OPEN 1,1,0
250 PRINT CHR$(147)
260 POKE 54296,15
270 PRINT SPC(10) "LIGHT AND SOUND SHOW"
280 REM ****************
290 REM *** READ TAPE ***
300 REM ****************
310 GET #1,AA$,BB$,CC$,BO$
320 REM ******************
330 REM *** END OF FILE? ***
340 REM ******************
350 IF ST = 64 THEN GOTO 570
360 AA = ASC(AA$)
370 BB = ASC(BB$)
380 CC = ASC(CC$)
390 DD = ASC(B0$)
400 REM ***********************
410 REM *** CHANGE BORDER COLOR ***
420 REM ************************
430 POKE 532280,AA:POKE 53281,BB
440 REM ****************
450 REM *** PLAY MUSIC **
460 REM *****'***********
470 FOR X = 54272 TO 54295: POKE X,0:NEXT X
```

24

```
480 POKE 54277,BB
490 POKE 54275,BB: POKE 54276,17
500 POKE 54272,CC: POKE 54273,DD
5:20 REM ***-*********************************
53 REM *** HOLD NOTES RANDOM PERIOD OF"TIME *
540 REM **********************************
550 FOR DE = 1 TO INT(99 * RND(1) ): NEXT DE
560 GOTO 310
570 CLOSE 1
580 POKE 53280,254: POKE 53281,246
590 END
READY.
```

7

Medical History

Accurate medical records can be an important asset for every family. They may come in handy in case of sudden illness. If a family member suffers a severe allergic reaction, the emergency room staff may need to know the current medications the person has been taking. Would you be able to provide this information in the high-stress environment of a trauma center? In another instance, you may need only to provide a printout of Grandma Shelly's file to make the doctor's job easier.

The personal computer will make the collecting and sorting of such medical information easy, through writing to cassette tape or disk. The following Medical Record program uses some of the special characteristics of the Commodore 64 computer. Namely, the video screen is live. That means anything displayed on the screen can be read by the Commodore 64 and sent wherever you want it to go. It will soon be clear what we mean.

At the start of the program, you have a menu giving two choices:

1. READ RECORD.
2. WRITE RECORD.

Since we don't yet have any medical records yet, we'll ENTER a "2". That done, the screen clears and prints the Medical Form. At each question mark prompt, enter the appropriate information:

Name

Date of Birth

Known Allergies

And so on. After the last bit of information is entered, the Commodore 64 computer will one you to press the PLAY and RECORD buttons on the Datasette recorder. If this is the first time you're saving a file, make sure there's a blank, re-wound tape ready to store the new information.

Wait patiently while the program saves the data to tape. Once that's accomplished, the screen will clear and print the menu. Do you to check the file for accuracy, or update current medications? If so:

1. Rewind the cassette tape.
2. Press the PLAY button.
3. Enter menu selection "1".

The screen will clear and display the medical record and the file in a matter of moments. But things are much different at this point. Remember we said the screen was live? You'll see a question mark prompt in front of the first character of the person's name. At this point, if you hit. RETURN, that name will be saved exactly as is. If the name is misspelled, use the editing keys to correct it. Once you hit RETURN, whatever was printed on that line will be saved exactly as it was displayed On the screen.

When you hit RETURN, the question mark prompt jumps down to the Date of Birth line. Again, if you hit RETURN, the line will be saved exactly as it appeared on the screen. Add, delete, or leave as is each of the lines all the way down to Current Medications. Before you hit RETURN after Current Medications:

1. Rewind the tape in order to overwrite the old information.
2. Press the RECORD and PLAY buttons. It's at this point the information can be changed. Those cursor positions we mentioned place the old information on the right.

How the Program Works

Line 180 dimensions the variables.
Line 190 blanks the screen.
Lines 200 through 260 display the menu.
Line 310 compares the job selection stored in KE$ (KE). The number 1's ASCII code is "49". If the USER presses "1" the program goes to line 630 and reads back a stored medical file. Any response other than the number 1 will cause the program to continue on to line 330.

Lines 340 through 470 format the prompts which ask for Name, Birthdate, and so on. Each bit of information is sorted in its own string variable, e.g., Name in NA$. Line 490 opens the cassette channel for a write. One by one, each string variable is written to the tape.

When done writing, line 590 closes the channel.

Line 610 sends us back to the menu.

Reading a Medical Record

Line 630 opens the cassette channel for a read.

Lines 650, 680, 710, 740, 770, and 800 through 830 read the information stored on the tape. The INPUT #1, WHATEVER$ reads each string variable; the CO, RO variables and GO-SUBS locate the prompts.

Line 870 turns the cassette channel off.

Line 880 sends us to line 340.   "

Lines 920 through 1030 create strings of characters that we'll use to position the screen display.

Lines 920 through 950 build a string of 22 "cursor down" characters while lines 960 through 990 build a string comprised of 21 "cursor right" characters.

Later, we load the numeric variables RO and CO with values, and pull out part of these strings.

String and Numeric Variables

NA$ Retrieve or write person's name.

BI$ Retrieve or write person's birth date.

AL$ Retrieve or write known allergies.

VA$ Retrieve or write vaccinations, inoculations.

AI$ Retrieve or write ailments.

BO$ Retrieve or write bone fractures.

ME$ Retrieve or write current medications and dosage.

KE$(KE) Menu selection.

CO Which column to display.

RO Which row to display.

OO$ Move cursor right.

RD$ Move cursor down.

The Program

```
100 REM ****************************
110 REM *
120 REM *
130 REM *** MEDICAL HISTORY ****
140 REM *
150 REM *
160 REM ****************************
170 GOSUB 920
180 DIM NA$(21),B1$(10),AL$(21),VA$(21),A1$(21),B0$(21),ME$(21)
190 PRINT CHR$(147)
200 PRINT SPC(4)"MEDICAL RECORD"
210 PRINT
220 PRINT "1. READ RECORD"
230 PRINT
240 PRINT "2. WRITE RECORD"
250 PRINT
260 PRINT "CHOOSE 1 OR 2"
270 GET KE$: IF KE$ = "" THEN 270
280 PRINT CHR$(147)
290 KE = ASC(VE$)
300 REM *** DO JOB CHOSEN **
310 IF KE = 49 THEN GOTO 630
320 REM *** WRITE MEDICAL HISTORY ***
330 PRINT SPC(4) "MEDICAL RECORD"
340 CO = 0: RO = 2: GOSUB 1010
350 INPUT "NAME";NA$
360 CO = 0: RO = 5: GOSUB 1010
370 INPUT "BIRTHDATE";BI$
380 CO = 0: RO = 8: GOSUB 1010
390 INPUT "ALLERGIES"; AL$
400 CO = 0: RO = 11: GOSUB 1010
410 INPUT "VACCINATIONS"; VA$
420 CO = 0: RO = 14: GOSUB 1010
430 INPUT "AILMENTS"; A1$
440 CO = 0: RO = 17: GOSUB 1010
450 INPUT "BROKEN BONES";B0$
460 CO = 0: RO = 20: GOSUB 1010
470 INPUT "MEDICATIONS"; ME$
```

```
480 REM *** WRITE CASSETTE ***
490 OPEN 1,1,2
500 REM *** RECORD INFO ***
510 PRINT#1,NA$
520 PRINT#1,BI$
530 PRINT#1,AL$
540 PRINT#1,VA$
550 PRINT#1,AI$
560 PRINT#1,80$
570 PRINT#1,ME$
580 REM *** CLOSE CASSETTE CHANNEL ***
590 CLOSE 1
600 REM *** BACK TO MENU ***
610 GOTO 190
620 REM *** OPEN CASSETTE CHANNEL FOR READ ***
630 OPEN 1,1,0
640 REM *** READ MEDICAL RECORD ***
650 INPUT#1,NA$
660 CO = 6:RO = 2:GOSUB 1010
670 PRINT NA$
680 INPUT#1,BI$
690 CO = 11:RO = 5:GOSUB 1010
700 PRINT BI$
710 INPUT#1,AL$
720 CO = 11:RO = 8:GOSUB 1010
730 PRINT AL$
740 INPUT#1,VA$
750 CO = 14:RO = 11:GOSUB 1010
760 PRINT VA$
770 INPUT#1,A1$
780 CO = 10:RO = 14:GOSUB 1010
790 PRINT A1$
800 INPUT#1,B0$
810 CO = 14:RO = 17: GOSUB 1010
820 PRINT 80$
830 INPUT#1,ME$
840 CO = 13:RO = 20:GOSUB 1010
850 PRINT ME$
860 REM *** CLOSE RECORDER CHANNEL ***
870 CLOSE 1
```

```
880 GOTO 340
890 REM **********************
900 REM *** POSITION CURSOR ***
910 REM **********************
920 RO$ = ""
930 FOR X = 1 TO 22
940 RO$ = RO$ + CHR$(17)
950 NEXT X
960 CO$ = ""
970 FOR X = 1 TO 21
980 CO$ = Co* + CHR$(29)
990 NEXT X
1000 RETURN
1010 PRINT CHR$(19)
1020 PRINT LEFTS(RO$,RO);LEFT$(CO$,CO);
1030 RETURN
```

8.

Ghost Town Vampire Girls

Diana and her vampire sister, Tiger-breath, have invited you to visit their ghostly retreat. Once at their castle, you will find a succession of double doors. Behind one door is the very charming Lady Diana. Behind the other lurks her demented half-sister and vampire, Tiger-breath. On your adventure through the passageways of their ghostly retreat, you must choose from a succession of doors. Follow Diana as she lures you toward her boudoir. But be careful. Her blood-thirsty sister is stalking you. So choose a door and take a chance: On the lady, or the tiger.

This is a game of chance. Hit any key to try each of the sequence of doors; you'll soon know whether or not you've met your fate, or are getting closer to your rendezvous with Lady Di.

As you pick your way from room to room, you'll find clues as to Diana's presence. Don't pick the wrong room, or Tiger-breath will get you. If she does, and you want to try another round of castle-touring, hit any key.

How the Program Works

Line 170 sets the audio volume to maximum.

Lines 210 through 730 print the clues, room by room.

Line 800 flips a twelve-sided die to see whether you win or lose. Any number other than a 5 and you are OK.

If You Lose. . .

Line 1010 dramatically turns the border blood red.

Line 1020 blasts out a blunder sound.

Line 1060 is the "Press Any Key" subroutine.

Line 1080 starts a new game.

If You've Won!

Line 770 prints the victory message.

On Setting the Odds

Line 800 sets the win/lose odds. A random number between 0 and 12 is chosen. Your chances are 1 out of 13 to lose. Change the magic number to 24, and the odds of success turn in your favor, to 25 to 1. But drop the number to 3 and you have only a 1-in-4 chance of finding the lucky lady.

The WAIT Subroutine

Line 860 sets ATTACK/DELAY.

Line 880 sets the pulse width.

Line 890 sets the waveform.

Line 940 halts the program while it waits for a key to be pressedn any key, other than the RUN/STOP key. Until one of the keys is pressed, the program loops at line 940, patiently waiting for you to do something.

Sound Effects Subroutine

Line 840 starts a loop that clears the voice registers.

Line 920 will delay while the variable DE counts from 1 to 50. It's during this delay that the musical note plays. Increase the delay from 40 to 100 and the note plays for a longer duration. Decrease the delay, say from 40 to 10, and the note plays for a shorter period of time, almost a pip. Following the DELAY loop, the NEXT LOOP sends us back for the next musical note.

String and Numeric Variables

DE Length of delay in music routine.
NUM Random number to select win/lose odds.
CO Counts off each voice register, 54272 to 54295, as we clear it.
KE$ Has any key been pressed?

The Program

```
100 REM *********************************
110 REM *
120 REM *
130 REM * GHOST TOWN VAMPIRE GIRLS *
140 REM *
150 REM *
160 REM *********************************
170 POKE 54296,15
180 PRINT CHR$(147):REM CLEAR SCREEN
190 PRINT SPC(12) "VAMPIRE GIRLS"
200 PRINT:PRINT
210 PRINT "ENTER THE CASTLE KEEP. THE DOOR'S NOT"
220 PRINT "LOCKED. YOU CAN FAINTLY HEAR HER SING"
230 PRINT "A BAWDY LOVE BALLAD. ENTER."
240 GOSUB 800
250 PRINT "SAFE INSIDE, ANOTHER SET OF DOORS."
260 PRINT "HER CLOAK LIES ON THE STONE FLOOR"
270 PRINT "STILL ALIVE WITH THE SCENT OF HER"
280 GOSUB 800
290 PRINT "THE TROPHY ROOM. STAG AND DEER HEADS"
300 PRINT "A SILK BLOUSE RESTS ON A BEARSKIN RUG"
310 GOSUB 800
320 PRINT "THE DEN, WHERE SHE COUNTS GOLD COINS,
330 PRINT "TOYS WITH HANDFULS OF RUBIES AND"
340 PRINT "SAPPHIRES. HER VOICE SOUNDS CLOSER."
350 GOSUB 800
```

```
360 PRINT "A ROSE GARDEN IN BLOOM. THE SKULL AND"
370 PRINT "BLEACHED BONES OF AN UNLUCKY SUITOR."
380 PRINT "WILL YOU BE THE NEXT TO DIE?"
390 GOSUB 800
400 PRINT "FEASTING HALL LINED WITH THE SHIELDS"
410 PRINT "OF BRAVE KNIGHTS WHO DIED TRYING TO"
420 PRINT "SATISFY HER WICKED THIRST. . ."
430 GOSUB 800
440 PRINT "'JUST BEYOND THE DOOR, SHE PURRS...'"
450 PRINT "'COME PLEASE ME. JUST ONE MORE DOOR.'"
460 PRINT "'DON'T BE AFRAID OF THAT NASTY TIGER'"
470 GOSUB 800
480 PRINT "THE BEDROOM. EMPTY. SHE LIED."
490 PRINT "SHE'S PRONE TO THAT YOU KNOW. BUT"
500 PRINT "THERE IS ANOTHER SET OF DOORS, THOUGH."
510 GOSUB 800
520 PRINT "A SECRET PASSAGE TO THE WINE CELLAR."
530 PRINT "CASKS OF HEARTY RED WINE. RATS SCURRY"
540 PRINT "AT YOUR FEET, MOCKING YOU." 550 GOSUB 800
560 PRINT "THE DUNGEON. AN OLD BEGGAR IN RAGS"
570 PRINT "CACKLES. POINTS A GRIMY FINGER AT YOU"
580 PRINT "ANOTHER OF HER LOVER—BOYS,EH?"
590 GOSUB 800
600 PRINT "SHARPEN YOUR SWORD? HOW DOES ONE"
610 PRINT "COOK TIGER MEAT?"
620 PRINT "SEARCH THE TOWER. LOOK BY THE WINDOW."
630 PRINT "HER LONG WHITE DRESS LEFT AS A CLUE."
640 PRINT "MADAME PLAYS HARD TO GET."
650 GOSUB 800
660 PRINT "A COOK FIRE ROARS IN THE KITCHEN, A"
670 PRINT "ROAST SPUTTERS ON THE SPIT. DINNER"
680 PRINT "FOR TWO?"
690 GOSUB 800
700 PRINT "STEP OVER THE DEAD WARRIOR. DIANA HAS"
710 PRINT "KILLED MORE MEN THAN THE BLACK KNIGHT"
720 PRINT "OF WODIN—BAGEN. PRESS ON."
730 PRINT "SUCCESS!"
740 GOSUB 830
750 REM *** WE HAVE A WINNER! ***
760 PRINT:PRINT:PRINT
```

```
770 PRINT SPC(15)"YOU WIN!"
780 GOSUB 800:GOTO 170
790 REM *** WON OR LOST? ***
800 LET NUM = INT(12*RND(1))
810 REM *********************
820 REM *** SOUND EFFECTS ***
830 REM *********************
840 FOR CO = 54272 TO 54295: POKE CO,0:NEXT
850 REM *** SET ATTACK/DECAY & SUSTAIN/RELEASE ***
860 POKE 54277,88:POKE 54278,0
870 REM *** SET PULSE WIDTH ***
880 POKE 54275,8
890 POKE 54276,17
900 REM *** PLAY A NOTE ***
910 POKE 54272,66:POKE 54273,75
920 FOR DE = 1 TO 50:NEXT
930 IF NUM = 5 THEN GOTO 1010
940 GET KE$: IF KE$="" THEN 940
950 PRINT CHR$(147)
960 RETURN 970 REM ***************
980 REM *** YOU LOSE ***
990 REM ***************
1000 REM *** BORDER RED ***
1010 POKE 53280,2
1020 POKE 54272,100:POKE 54273,100
1030 PRINT:PRINT:PRINT
1040 PRINT SPC(8) "SORRY OLD BOY, YOU LOSE!"
1050 REM *** RETURN SCREEN TO NORMAL COLOR ***
1060 GET KE$: IF KE$ = "" THEN 1060
1070 POKE 53280,14
1080 GOTO 180
READY
```

9.

Beowulf versus Grendel

Beowulf the warrior-man meets Grendel the monster on the field of battle. You are heroic Beowulf. Hear the trumpets blare! Grendel is the hideously ugly monster. He has been terrorizing the village, killing cattle, torching homes and barns, stealing beautiful maidens, and murdering good men in cold blood.

You, brave fellow that you are, have volunteered to slay this evil monster Grendel. Grendel is the red player; you, the yellow. Use the joystick to maneuver across the field. Push the trigger button to slash out with your light saber. The first warrior to make twenty hits on the other wins.

How the Program Works

Line 170 blanks the screen.

Lines 180 and 190 define the functions that read the joystick and trigger button.

Line 200 defines the numeric variables.

Line 210 assigns the string variable BL$ as consisting of 5 blank spaces. We'll be using this later to erase and update the score.

Line 240 creates a random number between 0 and 9.

Lines 250 through 340 take the random number and give it a plus or minus value, and then assign that value to the numeric variable X.

Line 350 takes the variable stored in X and adds it to Grendel's current horizontal position (GRE). If X is a positive number, Grendel will move to the right; if a negative number, will move to the left.

Lines 360 and 370 check to see if Grendel has wandered off to either side of his border. If so, he is dumped back into the center of the screen.

Lines 380 and 390 figure out how far apart the two players are. If more than 25 paces, then move Grendel nearer to Beowulf. These two seemingly insignificant lines are Grendel's brains. The bigger the number in " > 25" the dumber he is, and the smaller the number, the smarter he is.

Substitute

```
380 IF ABS(GRE — BEO) > 25 with
380 IF ABS(GRE — BEO) > 5
```

and see what happens.

Line 400 locates Grendel's image at its newly calculated position.

Line 410 slaps Grendel's light saber, in the form of a sprite image, into his right hand.

Line 420 moves the light saber one step towards Beowulf by poking the vertical position register with an ever increasing value.

Line 430 increments the variable that advances Grendel's light saber beam, but only if its value is less than 190. Rather briefly, in case you're not familiar with sprite graphics, to move a sprite from top to bottom, one pokes in a number between 0 and 230 into its vertical position register.

Line 440 restores the numeric variable DW to its top of the screen value of 90.

Line 450 resets the light beam's horizontal position register to the far left side of the screen. That way, the next time Grendel wants to strike out, he'll be ready.

Line 460 checks the sprite collision register to see whether Grendel managed to hit

Beowulf. If so, the score is incremented by five points and the program GOSUBS to display the updated score as well as making a little noise.

Line 470 sets the odds for the game. As it stands, Grendel gets to take two shots at Beowulf for each one of his.

Line 490 zeroes the odds. Once Grendel has slashed out twice, it's Beowulf's turn.

Lines 500 and 510 read the joystick and the trigger button, assigning the resulting readings to numeric variables.

Lines 520 and 530 move Beowulf to the right or to the left, depending on which direction you've yanked the joystick.

Line 540 increments the numeric variable that controls Beowulf's light saber. If you've pressed the trigger button, the sprite moves from the bottom to the top of the screen. Once at the top, the flag that said, "fire the light saber", is switched off.

Lines 560 and 570 keep incrementing Beowulf's vertical light beam position until it reaches the top of the screen.

Line 600 checks to see if Beowulf struck Grendel. When he does, the score is incremented by five points. Also, the program GOSUBs to display the updated score.

Line 630 moves the cursor to the top right corner of the screen.

Line 640 displays Grendel's latest score.

Line 650 clears the sprite collision register.

Line 660 assigns values to the variables we'll use to plug a pitch into the sound effect routine.

Line 680 moves the cursor to the top right corner of the screen. Line 690 displays Beowulf's latest score.

Line 700 clears the sprite collision register.

Line 710 plugs a pitch into the two variables we'll use to create a sound effect.

Line 720 erases old values in the voice registers.

Lines 730 through 760 create a sound.

Lines 810 through 1360 create the sprite images.

Line 830 points to each image.

Lines 850 through 900 load the image into RAM from their DATA statements.

Lines 1020 through 1360 are the data statements holding each of the three images. Notice how both Grendel and Beowulf share the same light saber image.

String and Numeric Variables

FL Beowulf's light beam striking out?
UP Beowulf's light beam's vertical position.
GRE Grendel's horizontal position.
BBQ Beowulf's horizontal position.

GD Beowulf's score.

BD Grendel's score.

BL$ Five blank spaces used as an old score eraser.

NU A random number between O and 9.

JS Joystick reading.

TR Trigger button reading.

LOW/HI Pitch of the sound we'll create.

CL Counts off the voice registers, 54272 to 54295, as zeroed.

IM Sprite image being loaded into RAM.

CO Counts off each sprite 63 bytes to be loaded into RAM.

BY Individual byte's value.

The Program

```
100 REM *****************************************
110 REM *
120 REM *
130 REM *** BEOWULF VERSUS GRENDEL ***
140 REM *
150 REM *
160 REM ****************************
170 PRINT CHR$(147)
180 DEF FN JOY(X) = 15 - (PEEK(56320) AND 15)
190 DEF FN BUT(X) = 16 - (PEEK(56320) AND 16)
200 FL=0:UP =200:DW=70:GRE=130:BE0=130:GD=0:B =0
210 BL$ = "     "
220 GOSUB 810
230 REM * RANDOM NUMBER *
240 NU = INT(9 * RND(1))
250 IF NU = 0 THEN LET X = 10
260 IF NU = 1 THEN LET X = -10
270 IF NU = 2 THEN LET X = 20
280 IF NU = 3 THEN LET X = -20
290 IF NU = 4 THEN LET X = 5
300 IF NU = 5 THEN LET X = -5
310 IF NU = 6 THEN LET X = 25
320 IF NU = 7 THEN LET X = -25
330 IF NU = 8 THEN LET X = 15
340 IF NU = 9 THEN LET X = -15
350 GRE = GRE + X
```

```
360 IF GRE > 247 THEN GRE = 60
370 IF GRE < 20 THEN GRE = 100
380 IF ABS(GRE - BEO) > 25 THEN GRE = BEO
390 IF ABS(BEO - GRE) > 25 THEN GRE = BEO
400 POKE 53248,GRE
410 POKE 53250,GRE + 1
420 POKE 53251,DW
430 IF DW < 190 THEN DW = DW + 35:GOTO 420
440 DW = 90
450 POKE 53250,1
460 IF PEEK(53278) = 6 THEN BD = BD + 5:BOSUB 630
470 ODDS = ODDS + 1: IF ODDS > 1 THEN 490
480 GOTO 240
490 ODDS = 0
500 JS = FN JOY(0)
510 TR = FN BUT(0)
520 IF JS = 4 THEN IF BEO > 50 THEN BED = BEO 8:POKE
53252,BE0
530 IF JS = 8 THEN IF BEO < 247 THEN BEO = BEO + 8:
POKE 53252,BEO
540 IF TR = 16 THEN FL = 1:POKE 53254,BE0
550 IF FL = 1 THEN UP = UP - 25:POKE 53255,UP
560 IF UP < 75 THEN 580
570 GOTO 500
580 FL = 0:UP = 200
590 POKE 53254,1
600 IF PEEK(53278) = 9 THEN GD = GD + 5:GOSUB 680
610 GOTO 240
620 REM * COLLISION *
630 PRINT CHR$(19)
640 PRINT "GRENDEL ";BD;BL$
650 POKE 53278,0
660 LOW = 134:HI = 33
670 GOTO 720
680 PRINT CHR$(19)
690 PRINT SPC(20) "BEOWULF ";GD;BL$
700 POKE 53278,0
710 LOW = 97:HI = 56
720 FOR CL = 54272 TO 54295:POKE CL,O:NEXT CL
730 POKE 542729,LOW:POKE 54273,HI
```

```
740 POKE 54275,8 :POKE 54278,8
750 POKE 54276,17:POKE 54277,88
760 POKE 54296,12
770 RETURN
780 REM ************************
790 REM * SET-UP SPRITE
800 REM ************************
810 POKE 53269,0
820 REM *** ASIGN SPRITE POINTERS ***
830 POKE 2040,192:POKE 2041,193:POKE 2042,194:POKE
2043,193
840 REM *** STORE IMAGES *** '
850 FOR IM = 0 TO 2
860 FOR CO = 0 TO 62
870 READ BY
880 POKE (192 + IM) * 64 + CO,BY
890 NEXT CO
900 NEXT IM
910 REM *** PAINT SPRITES ***
920 POKE 53287,2:POKE 53288,2:POKE 53289,7:POKE
53290,7
930 REM *** SWITCH-ON FOUR SPRITES ***
940 POKE 53269,15
950 REM *** HORIZONTAL POSITIONS ***
960 POKE 53248,GRE:POKE 53250,1:POKE 53252,BEO:POKE
53254,1
970 REM *** VERTICAL "Y" POSITIONS ***
980 POKE 53249,DW:REM * GRENDEL *
990 POKE 53253,UP:REM * BEOWULF *
1000 RETURN
1010 REM *** GRENDEL ***
1020 DATA 0,255,0,0,255,0
1030 DATA 255, 255,255,255,255, 255,255,255
1040 DATA 0,255,0,0,255,0
1050 DATA 0,255,0,0,255,0
1060 DATA 255,255,255,255,255,255
1070 DATA 255,255,255,255,255,255
1080 DATA 0,255,0,0,255,0
1090 DATA 0,255,0,0,255,0
1100 DATA 255,255,255,255,255,255
```

```
1110 DATA 255,255,255,255,255,255
1120 DATA 255,255,255,0,0,0
1130 REM *** LIGHT SABER ***
1140 DATA 0,255,0,0,0,0
1150 DATA 0,255,0,0,0,0
1160 DATA 0,255,0,0,2,0
1170 DATA 0,255,0,0,0,0
1180 DATA 0,255,0,0,2,0
1190 DATA 0,255,0,0,0,0
1200 DATA 0,255,0,0,0,0
1210 DATA 0,255,0,0,0,0
1220 DATA 0,255,0,0,0,0
1230 DATA 0,255,0;0,0,0
1240 DATA 0,255,0
1250 REM *** BEOWULF ***
1260 DATA 255,255,255,255,255,255
1270 DATA 0,56,0,0,56,0
1280 DATA 255,255,255,255,255,255
1290 DATA 0,56,0,0,56,0
1300 DATA 255,255,255,255,255,255
1310 DATA 0,56,0,0,56,0
1320 DATA 255,255,255,255,255,255
1330 DATA 0,56,0,0,56,0
1340 DATA 255,255,255,255,255,255
1350 DATA 255,255,255,255,2559255
1360 DATA 255,255,255
```

10

Electronic Postage Meter

Unless you mail hundreds of letters a year, you probably don't have a postage scale within easy reach. That's no problem if you're just dashing off a quick letter to Aunt Bea, but what happens when you have to stuff more than a few sheets of typing paper into the envelope? It means a journey down to the long line at the Post Office where the nice man behind the counter weighs the letter, smiles, and says, "You need two more stamps, thank you very much. . ."

The inconvenience of driving downtown and having to waste time in line can be remedied easily enough with the following program. With it, simply tell the machine the weight of the paper you're mailing, for instance either 16- or 20-pound, how many sheets will go in the envelope, followed by the kind of envelope. That done, the correct postage will be displayed on the screen.

This postal scale/meter needs no maintenance and is as available as your keyboard. Remember to update with the new prices as the postage goes up.

How the Program Works

Line 170 blanks the screen.

Line 250 inputs which bond of paper you'll be figuring.

Lines 270 and 280 load the variable WE with the per-sheet weight of whichever bond you've selected. If you often find the need to mail photocopies, it might pay to weigh a sheet of both letter and legal size and modify the program to include those items.

Line 310 supplies the number of sheets to multiply the paper's weight by. The sum of all the sheets is stored in line 310's numeric variable, you guessed it, WE.

Lines 340 through 400 input the envelope's weight. In line 410, notice a business-sized envelope weighs about the same as a piece of 20-pound bond. If you unfold one of these envelopes and spread it flat on your desk, you'll see it's also the same size. A manila envelope, however, weighs about a full ounce. If you routinely send off those big padded mailers, have the different sizes weighed and modify the program to include them as an option.

Line 440 adds the weight of the mailer to that of the paper.

Line 460 figures out how many ounces will be mailed. The U.S. Postal Service rolls over any portion of an ounce to the next full ounce. For example, the USPS consider 4.1, as well as 4.9 ounces, to be 5 ounces. The math in line 460 does some quick footwork to roll over any portions to the next full ounce.

Line 480 charges 55-cents for the first ounce, 15-cents for each additional ounce, and stores that sum in the numeric variable PO.

Line 500 displays the required postage. Ugh, the glue on stamps tastes horrible. Even the taste of the self adhesive stamps turns the stomach.

Line 520 waits for a keystroke. Hit any key and figure the next letter, or the RUN/STOP and RESTORE keys to quit.

String and Numeric Variables

BO Weight of paper (e.g., 16-pound bond, 20-pound bond).

WE Weight of an individual sheet of paper.

NU How many sheets of paper are to be mailed.

EN Which type mailer to be used.

AD Weight of the mailer.

PO Amount of money needed (in stamps) to mail your correspondence.

The Program

```
100 REM ********************
110 REM *
120 REM *
130 REM * POSTAGE SCALE *
140 REM *
150 REM *
160 REM ********************
170 PRINT CHR$(147)
180 PRINT SPC(5) "POSTAL. SCALE"
190 PRINT
200 PRINT "WEIGHT OF PAPER":PRINT
210 PRINT "1. 16-POUND PAPER"
```

```
220 PRINT
230 PRINT "2. 20-POUND PAPER"
240 PRINT
250 INPUT BO
260 REM *** FIGURE WEIGHT OF SHEET OF PAPER ***
270 IF 80 = 1 THEN WE = . 128
280 IF BD = 2 THEN WE = . 16
290 PRINT
300 REM *** NUMBER OF SHEETS ***
310 INPUT "NUMBER OF SHEETS ";NU
320 WE = NU * WE
330 REM *** WEIGHT OF MAILER ***
340 PRINT: PRINT SPC(5) "MAILER SIZE"
350 PRINT
360 PRINT "1. BUSINESS SIZE ENVELOPE"
370 PRINT ·
380 PRINT "2. MANILLA"
390 PRINT
400 INPUT EN
410 IF EN = 1 THEN AD = .16
420 IF EN = 2 THEN AD = 1
430 REM *** TALLY WEIGHT ***
440 WE = WE + AD
450 REM *** ROLL OVER TO NEXT FULL OUNCE ***
460 IF WE ~ INT(WE) > 0 THEN WE = INT(WE) + 1
470 REM *** CALCULATE POSTAGE ***
480 PO = ( (WE - 1) * .15) + .55
490 PRINT
500 PRINT "POSTAGE = $";PO
510 REM *** WAIT FORPRESS ***
520 GET KE$ : IF KE$ = "" THEN 520
530 GOTO 170
```

11.
Form Letter Printer

Maybe the thought of actually sitting down and writing all those overdue letters to friends and relatives takes your breath away. Or, maybe you're looking for an easier way to send out your club or civic organization's mass mailing that tells the world about their latest achievements. No matter what the message, if there are five or more people to whom you want to send the same letter, this program will help remove the drudgery of communication.

How To Use the Program

To get started, write the letter with your favorite word processor. Assemble the names and addresses, keeping in mind a simple rule: There must be four lines per recipient. Here's an example of what business addresses would look like:

President
Middle Coast Publishing
P.O. Box 555
Hills, IA 52235
Vice President
Middle Coast Publishing
P.O. Box 555
Hills, IA 52235
Treasurer
Middle Coast Publishing
P.O. Box 555
Hills, IA 52235
END

Notice how "END" follows the mailing list. That's the signal to the Commodore 64 that the program has reached the end of the mailing list. It must be included.

Here's what home addresses look like:

John Smith
One Disk Drive
Sunnyvale, CA
(blank space followed by RETURN)

Joe Hacker
12.8 K Street
Cupertino, C-A
(blank space" followed by RETURN)
END

Notice how the fourth line in every address is made up of a blank space followed by a RETURN. That's so the computer can still count to four, and not mix two different addresses. Again, you see that the last word in the mailing list is "END". It must be included or the program will go off into never-never land, trying to read a cassette file that ended long ago.

With the letter and mailing list stored in separate files, LOAD and RUN the form letter printer program. When prompted, enter the letter's filename. Enter a carriage return, and the program will load whichever file is next in line on the tape. After the Commodore 64 loads the form letter into RAM, it will ask you for the name of the mailing list file. Once you enter a filename or carriage return, the program will print the name and address at the top of the page, followed by the form letter, and, finally, the "eject page" ASCII command. At the top of the page, the process repeats itself with the printing of the next name and address followed by the letter.

When all of the letters are printed, you'll be coached to insert an envelope. First, you'll have to rewind the cassette tape to the start of the mailing list so it can be read a second time. That done, tap any key and it's addressed. Slip in another envelope, tap a key, and so on, until all the envelopes are addressed. Then it's up to you to fold, stamp, and seal your project.

How the Program Works

Line 170 blanks the screen.
Line 180 dimensions the variables we'll use to pass information from the files to the printer via Commodore 64.
Line 190 assigns values to the numeric variables, and dumps any stray characters from the string variables assigned to the filenames.
Line 210 opens the channel to the printer.
Line 240 prompts you for the name of the form letter you are about to mass mail.
Line 260 opens the cassette file holding the letter.
Line 280 counts how many characters are read.
Line 290 reads one character at a time and stores them in an array so we can read them back later on in the program.
Line 310 watches for the end of the letter file.

Line 320 closes the,letter file, once we've read to the end.

Line 340 prompts you for the name of the file where you've stored all the names and addresses.

Line 350 opens the mailing list file.

Line 370 directs output to the printer.

Line 390 starts the loop that reads four lines at a time from the mailing list, and then prints those names and addresses.

Lines 440 through 460 read back the letters, which we conveniently stored in a string variable array.

Line 510 keeps an eye out for the end of the mailing list file. When reached, line 490 closes it.

Line 520 prompts you to hit a key, any key, but only after you've positioned an envelope in the printer, and rewound the tape so the recorder can replay the mailing list.

Line 550 reopens the mailing list. This time, instead of individually addressing the letters, we'll address the envelopes.

Lines 590 through 640 read the addresses four lines at a time and print them. Line 610 watches for the end of the file. Line

 650 ejects the envelope, so you don't have to struggle with form feed buttons.

Line 670 closes the mailing list file, while line 690 shuts off the out- put to the printer.

String and Numeric Variables

LT$ The form letter's filename.

MAIL$ The mailing list's filename.

ADD$ Line of characters, from mailing list, beingread.

TXT$ Individual characters, from form letter, being read.

CO Counts number of characters being read from form letter.

EJECT 12 is the ASCII code that causes the printer to eject a page.

The Program

```
100 REM **********************
110 REM
120 REM
130 REM ***** FORM LETTER PRINTER ***
140 REM
150 REM
160 REM **********************
170 PRINT CHR$(47)
180 DIM LT$(14), MAIL$(14), ADD$(40), TXT$(2048)
190 DIM BL$(40): BL$ =""
200 CO = (2): EJECT = 12:LT$ = "": MAIL$=""
210 OPEN 4,4
220 PRINT SPC(5) "FORM LETTER PRINTER"
230 PRINT:PRINT
240 INPUT "FORM LETTER FILE"; LT$
250 REM *** OPEN CASSETTE PILE ***
260 OPEN 1,1,0,LT$
270 REM * LOAD LETTER INTO RAM CHARACTER BY CHAR *
280 CO = CO + 1
290 GET #1,TXT$(CO)
300 PRINT TXT$(C0);
310 IF ST <> 64 THEN 280
320 CLOSE 1
330 PRINT
340 INPUT "MAILING LIST :";MAIL$
350 OPEN 1,1,0, MAIL$
360 REM *** SEND CHARACTERS TO PRINTER ***
370 CMD 4
380 REM *** READ FIRST ADDRESS ***
390 FOR Y = 1 TO 4
400 INPUT#1,ADD$
410 IF ADD$ = "END" THEN 500
420 PRINT#4,ADD$
430 NEXT Y
440 PRINT#4,CHR$(32)
450 FOR Y = 1 TO CO
460 PRINT#4,TXT$ (Y);
```

```
470 NEXT Y
480 PRINT#4,CHR$(EJECT);
490 GOTO 390
500 CLOSE 1: CLOSE 4
510 PRINT CHR$(147)
520 PRINT "1. REWIND TAPE":PRINT "2. INSERT
ENVELOPE": PRINT "TAP SPACE BAR"
530 GET KE$:IF KE$<> CHR$(32) THEN 530
540 REM ** REOPEN ADDRESS FILE ***
550 OPEN 1,1,0, MAIL$
560 OPEN 4,4
570 CMD 4
580 REM *** READ FIRST ADDRESS "*
590 FOR Y = 1 TO 4
600 INPUT#1ADD$
610 IF ADD= "END" THEN 640
620 REM *** PRINT IT ***
630 PRINT#4,BL$;ADD$
640 NEXT Y
650 PRINT#4,CHR$(EJECT)
660 GOTO 590
670 CLOSE 1
680 PRINT#4,CHR$(EJECT);
690 CLOSE 4
700 END
```

12.

Jet Jockey

Dateline: Blue skies over the Rhine River valley. The world is once again at war. You are strapped into the cockpit of a Tomcat F-14 fighter plane. Armed with air-to-air rockets, you monitor the radar screen, watching for the blips of attacking Soviet planes.

When one appears, jockey your plane to get a clear shot at Ivan. Each attack comes at a different speed.

Fly your plane with the joystick. Yank it left, and your plane banks to the left. Yank right, and the plane banks to the right. Press the trigger button to fire the rockets to defend yourself. One after the other, swarms of Red warplanes will come at you.

How the Program Works

Line 170 blanks the screen.

Lines 180 and 190 define the functions that we'll use to read the joystick and trigger button.

Lines 200 and 210 assign our variables.

Line 240 picks a random number between 0 and 8.

Line 260 starts a loop that will count from 25 to 230, but it will count in steps determined by the random number selected in line 240.

Line 270 takes the number from the above mentioned loop and plugs it into sprite number 1's horizontal position register. Every time the loop increments, the sprite moves right across the screen by how ever many positions the step command dictates.

Lines 280 and 290 assign a variable to the joystick and trigger button readings.

Lines 300 and 310 check that variable. If you cranked the joystick to the right or to the left, the sprite, whose image is your jet, will be moved accordingly.

Line 320 checks to see if the enemy jet is in range. If so, it's loaded with a missile, and its trigger button, the numeric variable FIRE, is turned on.

Line 330 moves the missile on its downward flight towards your plane. Line 340 holds the pitch of the explosion if the enemy missile blasts your fighter plane out of the sky.

Line 350 watches for the missile to flash past your plane, as it would should it miss the target. When that happens, the enemy missile is replaced at the top of the screen, but way off to the left and out of sight.

Line 360 checks to see if the missile scored a hit on your plane. If so, the program GOSUBS to line 450, where the explosion sound effect is located. When the program returns to line 360, we turn off the enemy missile, and hide it at the top and extreme left of the screen.

Line 370 reads the trigger button to see whether or not you've fired your missile. If so, the numeric variable FLAG is clicked on, and a missile is loaded under your wing.

Line 380 checks to see if FLAG is equal to 1. If so, the missile takes off towards the enemy plane in increments of 25.

Line 390 assigns the pitch of the explosion we'll hear if you blast the enemy fighter out of the sky.

Line 400 reads the sprite collision register to see whether or not you've hit the enemy. If so, then the program GOSUBS to the explosion sound effect. When it returns, the FLAG is turned off, and your missile is hidden at the top left of the screen.

53

Line 410 watches for your missile to fly right past the enemy. If you miss, the "fire my missile" FLAG is turned off.

Line 430 starts another flight of the enemy missile across the screen.

Lines 450 through 530 comprise the explosion sound effect subroutine. In detail, line 450 clears the voice registers of any old, and possibly invalid, settings.

Line 460 calls for a continuous tone.

Line 470 calls for noise, instead of a pure tone, and that's perfect for a good explosion sound.

Line 480 stuffs the pitch of the explosion into the tone registers.

Lines 490 through 510 decrement the volume, from maximum to zero, and pause for a beat, just for effect.

Lines 540 through 1090 set up the sprite graphics.

In detail, line 560 tells the voice chips where to look for each of the images.

Lines 580 through 630 load each of the three images into RAM.

Line 650 paints each of the sprites a different color.

Line 660 tells the video chip we'll be using four sprites.

Line 690 places each sprite in an appropriate horizontal position.

Similarly, lines 710 and 720 place each sprite in an appropriate vertical position.

Lines 750 through 1090, and their data statements, hold each sprite's image.

String and Numeric Variables

FLAG Good guys firing a missile.

FIRE Enemy jet firing a missile.

UP Good guys' missile's vertical position.

DOWN Enemy missile's vertical position.

WHITE Your jet's horizontal position.

MOVE Enemy jet's horizontal position.

SPEED How fast enemy jet flies across screen.

I Clears voice registers of old data.

LOW/HI Pitch of explosion.

VO Volume of explosion as it decrements from 15 to 0.

DE Period of time each VO is held (DElay).

IMAGE A single sprite's image as it's loaded into RAM.

COUNT A single byte of each sprite's image as it's loaded intoRAM.

BYTE The value of a byte as a sprite is loaded into RAM.

JS Joystick reading.

TRIG Trigger button reading.

The Program

```
100 REM **********************
110 REM *
120 REM *
130 REM JET JOCKEY GAME
140 REM *
150 REM *
160 REM **********************
170 PRINT CHR$(147)
180 DEF FN JOY(X)= 15 - (PEEK(56320) AND 15)
190 DEF FN BUT(X) = 16 - (PEEK (56320) AND 16)
200 FLAG = 0: FIRE = 0: UP =200:DOWN = 75
210 WHITE = 130
220 GOSUB 540
230 REM *** BEGIN GAME ***
240 LET SPEED = INT(8* RND(1))
250 IF SPEED < 2 THEN SPEED = 15
260 FOR MOVE = 25 TO 230 STEP SPEED * 2
270 POKE 53248, MOVE
280 JS = FN JOY(0)
290 TRIG = FN BUT(0)
300 IF JS = 4 THEN IF WHITE > 50 THEN WHITE = WHITE - 8:POKE
53252,WHITE
310 IF JS = 8 THEN IF WHITE < 250 THEN WHITE = WHITE + 8: POKE
53252,WHITE
320 IF ABS(WHITE - MOVE)< 15 THEN POKE 53250,
MOVE:FIRE = 1
330 IF FIRE = 1 THEN DOWN =DOWN + 25 :POKE 53251,
DOWN
340 IF FIRE = 1 THEN LOW = 97: HI = 8
350 IF DOWN > 200 THEN DOWN = 60:POKE 53250,1
360 IF POKE(53278) = 6 THEN GOSUB 450: FIRE = 0:POKE
53250,1
370 IF TRIG = 16 THEN FLAG = 1: POKE 53254, WHITE
380 IF FLAG = 1 THEN UP = UP - 25:POKE 53255,UP
390 IF FLAG = 1 THEN LOW = 12: HI = 69
400 IF PEEK(53278) = 9 THEN GOSUB 450:FLAG = 0:POKE
53254,1
410 IF UP <10 THEN FLAG = 0:UP = 200
420 NEXT MOVE
```

```
430 GOTO 240
440 REM *** EXPLOSION SOUND EFFECT ***
450 FOR I = 54272 TO 54295:POKE I,0:NEXT I
460 POKE 54278,240
470 POKE 54275,8 :POKE 54276,129
480 POKE 54272,LOW:POKE 54273,HI
490 FOR VO = 15 TO 0 STEP -1
500 POKÍE 54296,VO
510 FOR DE = 1 TO 20:NEXT DE:NEXT VO
520 POKE 53278,0
530 RETURN
540 POKE 53269,0
550 REM *** ASSIGN SPRITE POINTERS ***
560 POKE 2040,192:POKE 2041,193:POKE 2042,194:POKE
2043,193
570 REM *** STORE IMAGES ***
580 FOR IMAGE = 0 TO 2
590 FOR COUNT = 0 TO 62
600 READ BYTE
610 POKE (192 + IMAGE) * 64 + COUNT,BYTE
620 NEXT COUNT
630 NEXT IMAGE
640 REM *** PAINT SPRITES ***
650 POKE 53287,2:POKE 53288,7:POKE 53289,7:POKE
53290,5
660 REM *** SWITCH ON FOUR SPRITES ***
670 POKE 53269,15
680 REM *** HORIZONTAL POSITIONS ***
690 POKE 53248,10:POKE 53250,10:POLE 53252,
WHITE:POKE 55254,10
700 REM *** VERTICAL "Y" POSITIONS ***
710 POKE 53249,60:POKE 53251,60:REM *BAD GUY MISSILE
720 POKE 53253,200:POKE 53255,200
730 RETURN
740 REM *** ENEMY PLANE ***
750 DATA 0,1,128,0,3,128
760 DATA 0,7,128,192,7,128
770 DATA 192,7,128,192,7,128
780 DATA 192,7,128,192,7,128
790 DATA 255,255,255,255,255,255
```

```
800 DATA 255,555,255,255,255,555
810 DATA 192,7;128,192,7,128
820 DATA  192,7;128,192,7,128
830 DATA 192,7,128,0,7,128
840 DATA 0.3,128,0,1,128
850 DATA 0,0,0
860 REM *** THE MISSILE ***
870 DATA 0,24,0,0,24,0
880 DATA 0,24,0,0,24,0
890 DATA 0,24,0,0,24,0
900 DATA 0,24,0,0,24,0
910 DATA 0,24,0,0,24,0
920 DATA 0,0,0,0,0,0
930 DATA 0,0,0,0,0,0
940 DATA 0,0,0,0,0,0
950 DATA 0,0,0,0,0,0
960 DATA 0,0,0,0,0,0
970 DATA 0,0,0
980 REM *** GOOD GUY'S PLANE ***
990 DATA 0,0,0,0,16,0
1000 DATA 0,56,0,0,56,0
1010 DATA 0,56,0,255,255,255
1020 DATA 255,255,255,255,255,255
1030 DATA 255,255,255,255,255,255
1040 DATA 0,56,0,0,56,0
1050 DATA 0,56,0,0,56,0
1060 DATA 0,56,0,0,56,0
1070 DATA 0,56,0,0,56,0
1080 DATA 0,56,0,0,255,0
1090 DATA 0,255,0
```

13.

Bridge Buster

Bridge Buster is a war game. You are behind enemy lines with one hundred pounds of (C-4 plastic explosives. Your mission: Blow up the bad guys' bridge. There are a number of complications.

First, you have to use at least five pounds, and no more than one hundred pounds of the C-4 you infiltrated with.

Second, even though you've been specially trained in using explosives, you don't know how many pounds it will take to drop this span into the gulch. You'll have to guess.

If you use too much, you'll blow away yourself and your buddies in addition to the bridge. These days there's little glory in being a posthumous hero. On the other hand, if you don't place a big enough charge, there will be a bang, but little else. If you have any explosives left, you can try again. But don't react out of frustration and overdo it.

To help you along, there will be clues, such as "Not quite enough", "Way off", as well as a tally of just how many pounds of explosives you've expended so far. By the way, each bridge is different. N 0 two ever require the same charge. That's because a random number determines the target figure.

Good luck. Should you or your commando force be killed, captured, or identified, we'll be sure to read about it in the papers.

How the Program Works

Line 170 blanks the screen.

Line 190 chooses how many pounds of explosives are needed to blow up the bridge.

Line 240 asks for your estimate of pounds needed to bring down the bridge.

Lines 250 and 260 make sure at least five pounds and no more than one hundred are used. Otherwise, you have to start over.

Lines 290 through 330 match how much you estimated against how many pounds Were actually needed.

Line 350 keeps track of how many pounds have been exploded.

Lines 360 and 370 end the program if all explosives are used up.

Lines 430 through 450 display the "Out of explosives" message on the screen.

Lines 500 through 570 create the explosion sound effect.

In detail, line 500.Clears the voice registers.

Line 510 calls for a constant tone.

Line 520 chooses a standard pulse, but with noise instead of pure tone. Here you'd usually see a 17 or 33 poked into the register instead of a 129. That's because we want to simulate an explosion and not a piano concert.

Line 530 supplies a lower octave note, just right for a bang.

Lines 540 through 560 decrement the volume.

String and Numeric Variables

CH Your estimate of pounds needed.

SU Pounds explosives left.

NE Pounds necessary to blow up bridge.

VO Volume (loudness) of the sound produced.

DE Loop counter used as time delay.

The Program

```
100 REM ********************
110 REM *
120 REM *
130 REM *** BRIDGE BUSTER ***
140 REM *
150 REM *
160 REM ********************
170 PRINT CHR$(147)
180 REM *** DETERMINE POUNDS NEEDED * * *
190 LET NE = INT(10 * RND(1)) + 1
200 NE = NE * NE:IF NE <5 THEN NE = 5
210 SU = 100
220 PRINT SPC(5) "NEW BRIDGE"
230 PRINT "POUNDS C4 REMAIN"
240 PRINT "HOW BIG OF A CHARGE?";:INPUT CH
250 IF CH < 5 THEN PRINT AT LEAST 5 POUNDS":GOTO 230
260 IF CH > 100 THEN PRINT NO MORE THAN 100":GOTO 230
270 GOSUB 500
280 PRINT:PRINT
290 IF (NE - CH) > 20 THEN PRINT "WAY OFF! MORE
EXPLOSIVES": GOTO 340
300 IF NE - CH > 5 THEN PRINT "NOT ENOUGH": GOTO 340
310 IF NE - CH < 5 THEN IF NE - CH = 1 THEN PRINT
"RIGHT ON THE MONEY": GOTO 390
320 IF NE - CH < 10 THEN PRINT "BRIDGE BLOWN AWAY'!
GOOD JOB TROOPIE":GOTO 390
330 IF CH - NE > 10 THEN PRINT"BLAMMO' BLEW AWAY YOU
AND THE BRIDGE":GOTO 390
340 FOR DE = 1 TO 2000:NEXT DE
350 LET SU = SU - CH
360 IF SU < 5 THEN GOTO 430
370 IF SU 4 < NE THEN GOTO 430
380 GOTO 230
390 FOR DE = 1 TO 2000:NEXT DE
400 REM *** PLAY ANOTHER GAME ***
410 GOTO 170
420 REM *** OUT OF EXPLOSIVES ***
430 PRINT"ONLY ";SU:" POUNDS LEFT"
```

```
440 PRINT
450 PRINT"NEEDED ";NE;"POUNDS"
460 GOTO 390
470 REM ******************
480 REM *** EXPLOSION ***
490 REM ******************
500 FOR I = 54272 TO 54295:POKE I,0:NEXT I
510 POKE 54278,240
520 POKE 54275,8:POKE 54276,129
530 POKE 54272,12:POKE 54273,69
540 FOR VO = 15 TO 0 STEP - 1
550 POKE 54296,VO
560 FOR DE = 1 TO 20:NEXT DE:NEXT VO
570 RETURN
```

14.

44 Magnum Russian Roulette

Russian Roulette is a deadly game of chance where one holds a revolver against the temple and pulls the trigger. There are five empty chambers and one loaded. It's the ultimate test of luck. This version is electronic, and somewhat safer. But, to spice things up, we'll pretend we're using a .44 Magnum, the world's most powerful handgun.

First, one bullet is loaded into one of the six empty chambers, and the cylinder is spun. It's spun at every turn. So, if five brave players have gone before you and heard click when they pulled the trigger, it doesn't necessarily mean you'll be the one to die. You may go on the first shot, or you may hang on until the seventeenth or eighteenth turn before finally making the transition to the next world.

To play, RUN the program. You'll see the game title and the number "1". At this point, player number one is up. Press any key to simulate pulling the trigger. If the first player's luck held, number two will come up on the screen, and the next poor soul will have to take his chance at cheating computer death. After each successful turn, the next number will come up, signaling the next turn.

How the Program Works

Line 90 blanks the screen.
Line 140 counts how many turns have been taken.
Line 180 spins the loaded cylinder.
Line 200 waits for someone to press a key.
Line 220 checks to see if the variable stored in SP is the same as stored in SH; if so, the gun fires. If not, line 240 sends us on to another turn.
Line 260 loads the six-cylinder revolver with one bullet.
Line 360 displays the lose statement.
Lines 380 through 450 simulate the sound of a gunshot. For a detailed explanation of how this subroutine works, consult the Bridge Buster program.
Line 520 clears old variable, and line 530 starts a new game.

String and Numeric Variables

NU Number of turns taken.
SP Random number that simulates spinning loaded cylinder.
SH Loaded cylinder.
KE$ Waits for any key to be pressed.
VO Decrementing pitch used in gunshot loop.
DE Duration sound of shot is held.

63

The Program

```
10 REM *********************
20 REM *
30 REM *
40 REM .44 MAGNUM GAME
50 REM *
60 REM *
70 REM *
80 REM *** BLANK SCREEN ***
90 PRINT CHR$(147)
100 PRINT SPC(10) ".44 MAGNUM GAME"
110 REM *** LOAD THE GUN ***
120 GOSUB 260
130 REM *** DISPLAY TURN ***
140 NU=NU+1
150 PRINT
160 PRINT SPC(16) ;NU
170 REM *** SPIN THE CYLINDER ***
180 SP=INT(6*RND(1) ) +1 )
190 REM *** PRESS ANY KEY ***
200 GET KES: IF ="" THEN 200
210 REM *** CYLINDER HAS BULLET? ***
220 IF SP=SH THEN GOTO 310
230 REM *** NEXT PERSON'S CHANCE ***
240 GOTO 140
250 REM *** LOAD ONE OF THE CYLINDERS ***
260 SH=INT(6*RND(1) )+1)
270 RETURN
280 REM
290 REM *** IF GUN FIRES ***
300 REM ********************
310 PRINT
320 REM *** BLACK CHARS. ***
330 PRINT CHR$(144)
340 REM *** BORDER RED ***
350 POKE 53280,2
360 PRINT SPC(9) "BETTER LUCK" NEXT TIME"
370 REM *** GUNSHOT ***
380 FOR I = 54272 TO 54295:POKE I,0:NEXT I
```

```
390 POKE 54278,240
400 POKE 54275,8:POKE 54276,129
410 POKE 54272,97:POKE 54273,8
420 FOR VO = 15 TO 0 STEP -1
430 POKE 54296,VO
440 FOR DE = 1 TO 20:NEXT DE
450 NEXT VO
460 REM *** PRESS ANY KEY ***
470 GET KE$: IF   = "" THEN 470
480 REM *** WHITE CHARACTERS ***
490 PRINT CHR$(5)
500 REM *** BLUE BORDER ***
510 POKE 53280,14
520 CLR
530 GOTO 90
```

15.

Oracle at Delphi

For thousands of years, people have been possessed with a desire to peek into the future. Even in these days of high technology, the popularity of psychics and science fiction continues. While the Oracle at Delphi is a game, it also can be taken seriously.

At university and other accredited paranormal research centers, the standard test for extrasensory perception, ESP, requires the subject to guess which card is next going to be drawn from a deck. The Oracle at Delphi, however, is no ordinary poker deck. In- stead of Kings, Queens, Jacks, and Aces, there are colored stars, pyramids and boxes.

One day, a research assistant noticed that some of the subjects who hadn't been considered psychic actually were. They had been predicting the order the cards would be drawn, such as, star, box, box, pyramid. The cards were coming up circle, star, box, box, pyramid. They were predicting the exact sequence; the only mistake was when that sequence actually began. In playing the oracle game, you might guess the order each of the sayings will appear on the TV. If your answers are wrong, check to be sure your pattern matches the machine's, but with one or two symbols out of synchrony.

Similarly, the oracle can be used as an ESP test. Have the subject become familiar with the sayings and ask him or her to predict which one will appear next.

This game can be used also to channel our intuition. Most of us have ESP, but we haven't used it in so long that the ability is hidden away, rusting from disuse. Naturally, when our ESP does break through, it's inconsistent and inaccurate—and hard to trust. How- ever, by using this game as an ESP test, or as a fortune telling session, our intuition muscles are exercised. With practice, intuition becomes consistent and reliable. While we may no longer need our intuition to sense the presence of a prowling saber-toothed tiger, we might instead focus the energy on how to best approach a grumbly spouse or make a business decision. For more insight on creatively using your intuition, see Ralph Blum's Book of Runes (New York: St. Martin's Press, 1983.

A final consideration: can brain power affect microprocessor decision making? To find out, concentrate. Envision which reading you want to come up next. Will it to do so. Hold your hand on the keyboard and let the Oracle cycle through a few turns. Of those few turns, how many times did your will win out over electronics? The answer may surprise you.

While this is a long program, all of it need not be entered in order to use it. That's because each set of text is like a color slide. Type in as many as you want until you get tired of typing. Fill in the rest at a later date. The program will run fine without them. Or, if you want to add even more sayings than the program provides, then add them. In order to do this, increase the random number located in line 180, from 24 to however many slides you add. Also, renumber program lines 1120 and 1130 to make room for the new slideshow.

How the Program Works

Line 170 blanks the screen.
Lines 190 and 200 branch to the various sayings.
Lines 210 through 230 represent how each of the sayings is displayed.
Line 240 sends us to the subroutine where the Commodore 64 waits for any key to be pressed.
Line 1120 comprises the wait routine for any key to be pressed.

The Program

```
100 REM **************
110 REM *
120 REM *
130 REM * ORACLE GAME *
140 REM *
150 REM *
160 REM **************
170 PRINT CHR$(147)
180 LET C=INT(30*RND(1))+1
190 ON C GOTO
210,250,290,330,370,410,450,490,520,560,600,640,680,720,760
200 ON C-15 GOTO 800,840,870,910,950,990,1030,1070,1100
210 PRINT SPC(5)"ARIES"
220 PRINT "A LUCKY SYMBOL FOR A WOMAN SHE WILL
RECEIVE FROM THE OPPOSITE SEX"
230 PRINT "FOR A MAN, JOY IN GIVING"
240 GOTO 1120
250 PRINT SPC(5) "DARK SIDE OF ARIES"
260 PRINT "LOSS OR MISPLACEMENT OF A VALUED OBJECT"
270 PRINT "FRIENDSHIP IN JEOPARDY"
280 GOTO 1120
290 PRINT SPC(5) "TAURUS"
300 PRINT "LOVE FULFILLED NOURISHMENT"
310 PRINT "MONEY WEALTH GOOD THINGS"
320 GOTO 1120
330 PRINT SPC(5) "DARK SIDE OF TAURUS"
340 PRINT "FRUSTRATION FINANCIAL"
350 PRINT "SETBACKS UNREQUITED LOVE"
360 GOTO 1120
370 PRINT SPC(5) "GEMINI"
380 PRINT "A PLEASUREABLE JOURNEY"
390 PRINT "TWO-WAY COMMUNICATION"
400 GOTO 1120
410 PRINT SPC(5) "DARK SIDE OF GEMINI"
420 PRINT "TRAVEL WILL INTERFERE WITH"
430 PRINT "PLANS TO DEEPEN LOVE"
440 GOTO 1120
```

```
450 PRINT SPC(5) "CANCER"
460 PRINT "FAMILY MATTERS RELATIVES CHILD"
470 PRINT "CHILDREN BIRTH"
480 GOTO 1120
490 PRINT SPC(5) "DARK SIDE OF CANCER"
500 PRINT "STRESSFUL NEWS ABOUT FAMILY"
510 GOTO 1120
520 PRINT SPC(5) "LEO"
530 PRINT "COMPLETE TRANSITION CHANGE OF ATTITUDE"
540 PRINT "PROSPERITY IF BLANK RUNE NEXT TURN"
550 GOTO 1120
560 PRINT SPC(5) "VIRGO"
570 PRINT "ONE YEAR'S TIME A HARVEST DUES PAID"
580 PRINT "EXPECT ATTORNEYS OR BANKERS"
590 GOTO 1120
600 PRINT SPC(5)"LIBRA"
610 PRINT "A UNION UNITING OF SPIRITS FOR A"
620 PRINT "COMMON GOAL. GIFTS BALANCE AND CENTERING"
630 GOTO 1120
640 PRINT SPC(5)"BLANK RUNE"
650 PRINT "MYSTERIES HIDDEN BY THE GODS"
660 PRINT "SECRETS BETTER LEFT UNTOLD"
670 GOTO 1120
680 PRINT SPC(5) "SCORPIO"
690 PRINT "UNEXPECTED MATERIAL WEALTH GAINS"
700 PRINT "SECRETS MYSTIQUE"
710 GOTO 1120
720 PRINT SPC(5) "DARK SIDE OF SCORPIO"
730 PRINT "YOU HAVE EXPECTED TOO MUCH AND WILL"
740 PRINT "BE DISAPPOINTED COURAGE"
750 GOTO 1120
760 PRINT SPC(5) "SAGITTARIUS"
770 PRINT "INCONVENIENCE ALL WILL WORK OUT ACCORDING
TO THE PLAN"
780 PRINT "MAYBE NOT YOUR PLAN, BUT ACCORDING TO
PLAN"
790 GOTO 1120
800 PRINT SPC(5) "CAPRICORN"
810 PRINT "INHERITANCE, A WILL, OLDER FOLKS"
820 PRINT "OF KINDLY DISPOSITION"
```

```
830 GOTO 1120
840 PRINT SPC(5) "DARK SIDE OF LIBRA"
850 PRINT "A GIFT"
860 GOTO 1120
870 PRINT SPC(5) "DARK SIDE CAPRICORN"
880 PRINT "WATCH OUT FOR MACHINES"
890 PRINT "BE AWARE MECHANICAL DEVICES CAN HARM YOU"
900 GOTO 1120
910 PRINT SPC(5) "AQUARIUS"
920 PRINT "BODILY WELFARE IMPORTANT NEW AGE
AWARENESS"
930 PRINT "FULLFILL HUMANISTIC MATTERS WATCH BIO
RHYTHMS"
940 GOTO 1120
950 PRINT SPC(5) "DARK SIDE AQUARIUS"
960 PRINT "YOU HAVE AN ENEMY THE NEXT RUNE"
970 PRINT "WILL TELL HOW TO DEAL WITH THEM"
980 GOTO 1120
990 PRINT SPC(5) "PISCES"
1000 PRINT "NEW AND STIMULATING ENVIRONMENT"
1010 PRINT "YOUR MIND WILL FLOURISH"
1020 GOTO 1120
1030 PRINT SPC(5) "DARK SIDE OF PISCES"
1040 PRINT "DON'T GET INVOLVED WITH"
1050 PRINT "ONES WHO WILL USE YOU"
1060 GOTO 1120
1070 PRINT SPC(5) "DARK SIDE OF LEO"
1080 PRINT "PROSPERITY CLEAN AIR FRESH WATER"
1090 GOTO 1120
1100 PRINT SPC(5) "DARK SIDE OF VIRGO"
1110 PRINT "ONE YEAR A HARVEST"
1120 GET KE$: IF KE$="" THEN 1120
1130 GOTO 170
```

16.

I-Chîng Coin Toss

The I-Ching, pronounced Yee-Ching, is an ancient Chinese method for determining one's fate. PreComputer Age practitioners used a set of tortoise-shell coins to determine a pattern of solid and broken lines. These patterns were analyzed and the verdict decreed.

We'll use the Commodore 64 to cast the patterns. You'll also need a compendium of I-Ching interpretations. There are a number of versions available in bookstores.

This computer version of the I-Ching prints two sets of color bars on the screen. They represent the result of tossing those ancient coins. Take the results and consult an I-Ching text to determine the answer to your question.

To toss the coins, RUN the program. It will display two sets of three broken and solid lines. These colored lines represent the tossing of the coins.

To toss again, hit any key. Every time a key is touched, the program will toss a new set of coins.

How the Program Works

Line 170 blanks the screen.

Line 180 moves the cursor to the top left corner of the TV screen.

Line 210 builds a display string made up of two graphics characters. Together, they equal a solid line.

Line 220 creates a display string made up of two graphics characters. Together, they equal a broken line.

Lines 240 through 260 build a string made up of nine "cursor right"characters.

Lines 270 and 280 add their nine characters to the solid and broken lines. That way, when displayed you'll see them in the center of the screen, instead of on the left side.

Lines 300, 360, 400, 440, 480, and 520 each choose a random number, either a 1 or a 2. In all cases, if the random number is a 1, then the solid line is displayed. If it's a 2, by default, then the broken line is displayed.

Line 560 waits for any key to be pressed, in order to draw the next set of coins tossed. When you're ready to quit, type in the letter "D".

String and Numeric Variables

SO$ A solid line made up of two graphics characters.
BR$ Broken line made up from two graphics characters.
A Random number used to simulate the toss of a coin.
X$ String comprised of fifteen "cursor right" characters.
KE$ Has any key been pressed?

The Program

```
100 REM *************************
110 REM *
120 REM *
130 REM *** I - CHING COIN TOSS ***
140 REM *
150 REM *
160 REM *************************
170 PRINT CHR$(147)
180 PRINT CHR$(28)
190 DIM X$(15)
200 REM *** BUILD SOLID AND BROKEN LINES **
210 SO$ = CHR$(162) + CHR$(162) + CHR$(162) +
CHR$(162)
220 BR$ = CHR$(162) + CHR$(187) + CHR$(172) +
CHR$(162)
230 REM *** BUILD CENTERING STRING ***
240 FOR X = 1 TO 15
250 X$ = X$+CHR$(29)
260 NEXT X
270 SO$ = X$ + SO$
280 BR$ = X$ + BR$
290 REM * RANDOM NUMBER SIMULATES HEADS OR TAILS *
300 LET A = INT(2*RND(1))+1
310 REM *** IF A = 1 THEN DRAW SOLID LINE ***
320 REM *** IF A = 2 DRAW A BROKEN LINE ***
330 IF A=1 THEN PRINT SO$: GOTO 360
340 PRINT BR$
350 REM *** FLIP COIN ***
360 LET A=INT(2*RND(1))+1
370 IF A=1 THEN PRINT SO$: GOTO 400
```

```
380 PRINT BR$
390 REM *** FLIP COIN ***
400 LET A=INT(2*RND(1))+1
410 IF A=1 THEN PRINT S0$: GOTO 440
420 PRINT BR$
430 REM *** FLIP COIN ***
440 LET A=INT(2*RND(1))+1
450 IF A=1 THEN PRINT SO$: GOTO 480
460 PRINT BR$
470 REM *** FLIP COIN ***
480 LET A=INT(2*RND(1))+1
490 IF A=1 THEN PRINT SO$: GOTO 520
500 PRINT BR$
510 REM *** FLIP COIN ***
520 LET A=INT(2*RND(1))+1
530 IF A=1 THEN PRINT SO$: GOTO 560
540 PRINT BR$
550 REM *** WAIT FOR KEY TO BE PRESSED ***
560 GET KE$:IF KE$ = "" THEN 560
570 IF KE$="D" THEN END
580 CLR
590 GOTO 170
```

17.

Adventure Dice Cast

Dungeon Masters can ease the task of assigning player strength, intelligence, karma, weapons, and other characteristics. This is a casting program for 4-, 6-, 8-, 10-, 12-, and 20-sided dice. Select a number from the menu to tell the program which dice to cast, and it instantly tells you the result. To cast a new number, choose the appropriate number representing the dice, and a new number is cast.

How the Program Works

Line 170 clears the screen.
Lines 200 through 370 format and display the menu.
Line 380 gets your choice. The Commodore 64 reads it in its ASCII code. The number 1, for instance, is 49 in ASCII.
Line 390 converts the ASCII roll to a branching routine.
Lines 450 through 550 roll the dice.
Lines 560 through 590 print the results and reload the dice.

String and Numeric Variables

RO$ The key pressed at menu and roll of the dice.
RO ASCII value of RO$

The Program

```
100 REM ****************
110 REM *
120 REM *
130 REM ** DICE CAST ***
140 REM *
150 REM *
160 REM ****************
170 PRINT CHR$(147)
180 PRINT
190 REM *** DISPLAY MESSAGE ***
200 PRINT SPC(2) "WHICH DICE TO CAST?"
210 REM *** DISPLAY MESSAGE ***
220 PRINT
230 PRINT "1. FOUR"
240 REM *** LOCATE CURSOR ***
250 PRINT
260 PRINT "2. SIX"
270 PRINT
280 PRINT "3. EIGHT"
290 PRINT
300 PRINT "4. TEN"
310 PRINT
320 PRINT "5. TWELVE"
330 PRINT
340 PRINT "6. TWENTY"
350 PRINT
360 REM *** CHOOSE A DICE ***
370 PRINT "SELECT NUMBER <1-6)";
380 GET RO$= IP RO$ = ""   THEN 380
390 RO = RSC(RO$) - 48
400 REM *** WHICH DICE ***
410 ON RO GOTO 450,470,490,510,530,550
420 REM *** IF WRONG KEV PRESSED, START OVER ***
430 GOTO 380
440 REM *** CAST DIE ***
450 RO=INT (4 * RND (1)) + 1
460 GOTO 560
470 RO= INT (6 * RND (1)} + 1
```

75

```
480 GOTO 560
490 RD = INT(8 * RND (121))+ 1
500 GOTO 560
510 RO= INT (10 * RND (1))
520 GOTO 560
530 RO = INT (12 * RND(1)) + 1
540 GOTO 560
550 RO = INT (20 * RND (1)) + 1
560 PRINT RD;
570 REM *** DISPLAY PROGRAM RESULTS ***
580 REM *** TOSS DICE AGAIN? ***
590 GOTO 380
```

18.

"R" Is for Red

Have you ever watched kids and grownups at a video arcade pouring a fortune's worth of quarters into games of intergalactic con- quest? Besides passing time and building hand-eye coordination, the gamers are acquiring an advantage unavailable to yesteryear's Neanderthal. With our readily accessible micros comes a new way of thinking, seeing, and communicating with the universe. And, although at first glance the R Is For Red game may appear similar to a well-known chain store home entertainment device, close scrutiny may reveal several dimensions that run deeper than any party game.

One of the discoveries in this dawn of high technology is that different hemispheres of the brain click in or out while different tasks are performed. In this light and sound cryptogram, there are two different dimensions in which the brain can operate. First is the conscious level, where one can remember—"Let's see, I saw a blue bar, two greens, and then a red."

But probably more important is the unconscious, or Zen, part—the Force part where one does not think about the tennis, jogging, or computer game strategy. One simply reacts without thinking, like so many of us do while performing a very familiar task. In "R" Is for Red, the color and music sequence is not remembered for its individual sight and sound, but rather is recalled as an entire block, or word if you will, made up of colors. The color bars are like an alphabet, where words are not spelled out with A to Z characters, but instead with patterns of blues, reds, greens, and yellows. As the colors flash on the screen, one does not dissect the word letter-by-letter but speed reads it as a word, phrase, and sentence.

Sound fascinating? Recall the film Close Encounters of the Third Kind, where an international team of scientists assembled at Devil's Tower to set up a music synthesizer/light show to communicate with space aliens. They communicated with blocks of color and sound in a high tech, computer-driven Esperanto. How many colors can your eyes and brain distinguish? Six or seven at one time is about average, but with practice, the galaxy is the limit.

One of the more sophisticated software aspects of this color cryptogram is how it uses graphics. While no animation is used, the program does make use of some of the unique qualities of the Commodore 64. In this case, speed. Instead of having to draw, undraw, then draw again every time the program needs to flash a color on the screen, the Commodore 64 simply needs to change the number stored in its sprite color register. This nifty device can change it in the blink of an eye. With this program, each of the four colors waits its turn for the poke that will call it to life. Each individual color remains painted for as long as the skill level delay loop allows.

When you play the game, you'll see SKILL LEVEL (1-5) at the top of the screen. At that point, hit any number from 1 to 5, with 1 being the slowest and easiest routine, and 5 being the fastest and toughest. By the way, 5 is also the most interesting, in terms of video and audio.

As the program puts you through your paces, it will flash colors on the screen, the color accompanied by its own musical note. When you see a blue bar, hit the letter B. Just touch the key; you won't need to hit RETURN.

R is for red, B is for blue, and Y is for yellow. When you respond with the correct key for the correct color, another color/ musical note will be added to the sequence. Get the picture?

How the Program Works

Line 90 clears the screen.

Line 120 prints the skill-level message, and the micro waits at line 1 30 for the choice. When a key from number 1 through 5 is typed, that key's ASCII code is compared to the table in lines 170 to 210. The appropriate skill value will be placed in the delay loop that determines how long the color bars will stretch on screen. Line 230 routes us to the beginning of the main program loop.

Line 470 picks a random number, any number between 1 and 4. That number is assigned a number. The first number will be between 1 and 4 and will tell the micro which of the four colors—red, blue, green, or yellow—to display. The second number, which keeps track of each particular color in the sequence, is assigned in each turn by line 510.

With a color chosen, and having told the micro where it is in the sequence, the program jumps to line 240.

Lines 240 to 310 hold the program loop where all the colors in the sequence so far are flashed on the screen. You will see all the previous colors you have remembered and keyed correctly, plus one addition to the pattern.

Lines 320 through 440 will test your memory of the sequence.

As each color comes up in its turn, lines 260 through 290 will send the program to the particular subroutine that paints that color. Then comes the musical note. Color and note are delayed for as long as was specified in the skill level. After the delay is satisfied, the sound is killed and the bar is painted black; then it's back to the main loop for the next color bar.

The loop knows how many colors were flashed on the screen and will wait for that many keystrokes. Each keystroke will be matched against the proper sequence. If you enter a color out of sequence, the program lumbers off to the blunder routine to let you know you aren't as quick or as smart as you once were.

The blunder routine, lines 860 through 950, plays a sour note, clears the value of all variables to Zero, and starts the game over.

However, if you haven't yet goofed in remembering the color sequence, the game will continue adding random color bars to the sequence.

One thought: Why not close both eyes and play by ear? Can you recall the sequence of musical notes? How about manual dexterity? Where is that "R"? Here is where one tries out the computer Zen mentioned earlier, remembering what we "saw" with the mind's eye, reaching out with that inner sanctum of grey matter that we little understand and so much crave to master. After all, that's why we're into microcomputers, right?

String and Numeric Variables

SK$/SK Skill level chosen. Holds ASCII number for 1 through 5. Then assigns one of five numbers, 25, 50, 100, 150, 200.

NU Number of color bars flashed on screen.

KE$ Which color bar. "R" is for red. Holds ASCII number for each letter.

AN Which color bar did you choose?

L1(2,5) Low register tone value.

H1(2,3) High register tone value.

ER Blanks the voice registers.

DE Holds value of sound delay loops.

TU(X) Where in sequence of color bars.

The Program

```
10 REM *******************
20 REM *
30 REM *
40 REM * "R" IS FOR RED *
50 REM *
60 REM *
70 REM *******************
80 GOSUB 990
90 PRINT CHR$(147)
100 PRINT SPC(14) "R IS FOR RED"
110 PRINT:PRINT
120 PRINT SPC(3) "SKILL LEVEL (1-5)"
130 GET SK$:IF SK$ = "" THEN 130
140 SK = ASC(SK$)
150 SK = SK - 48
160 PRINT CHR$(147)
170 IF SK = 1 THEN SK = 200
180 IF SK = 2 THEN SK = 100
190 IF SK = 3 THEN SK = 500
200 IF SK = 4 THEN SK = 10
210 IF SK = 5 THEN SK = 0
220 REM *** GET FIRST COLOR BAR ***
230 GOTO 450
240 FOR X = 1 TO NU
250 REM *** ASSIGN COLOR ***
260 IF TU(X) = 0 THEN GOSUB 570
270 IF TU(X) = 1 THEN GOSUB 640
280 IF TU(X) = 2 THEN GOSUB 710
290 IF TU(X) = 3 THEN GOSUB 780
300 REM *** DO NEXT COLOR BAR ***
310 NEXT X
320 FOR X=1 TO NU
330 REM *** DO NEXT COLOR BAR ***
340 GET KE$:IF KE$ = "" THEN 340
350 KE = ASC(KE$)
360 LET AN = TU(X)
370 REM *** TRANSLATE ANSWER TO ASCII
```

```
380 IF AN = 0 THEN AN = 66
390 IF AN = 1 THEN AN = 71
400 IF AN = 2 THEN AN = 89
410 IF AN = 3 THEN AN = 82
420 REM *** PATTERN VS PLAYER ***
430 IF KE <> AN THEN 860
440 NEXT X
450 NU = NU + 1
460 REM *** SELECT RANDOM COLOR ***
470 LET CO = INT(4*RND (1))
480 REM *** SAVE COUNT ***
490 LET X = NU
500 REM *** LABLE COLOR SEQUENCE ***
510 LET TU(X) = CO
520 REM *** TEST NEW COLOR ***
530 GOTO 240
540 REM ********************
550 REM *** PAINT COLOR SQUARE ***
560 REM ********************
570 POKE 53287,6:REM *** BLUE ***
580 Ll = 97:H1 = 8
590 L2 = 195:H2 = 16
600 L3 = 134:H3 = 33
610 GOSUB 1210
620 POKE 53287,0:REM *** BAR BLACK ***
630 RETURN
640 POKE 53288,5: REM *** GREEN ***
650 Ll = 143:H1 = 10
660 L2 = 30:H2 = 21
670 L3 = 60:H3 = 42
680 GOSUB 1210
690 POKE 53288,0
700 RETURN
710 POKE 53289,7: REM *** YELLOW ***
720 LI = 208:H1 = 18
730 L2 = 161:H2 = 37
740 L3 = 66:H3 = 75
750 GOSUB 1210
760 POKE 53289,0
770 RETURN
```

```
780 POKE 53290,2: REM *** RED ***
790 L1 = 47:H1 = 11
800 L2 = 95:H2 = 22
810 L3 = 191:H3 = 44
820 GOSUB 1210
830 POKE 53290,0
840 RETURN
850 REM *** BLUNDER ***
860 L1 = 255:H1 =8
870 L2 = 71:H2 = 6
880 GOSUB 1210
890 REM *** BORDER RED ***
900 POKE 53280,2
910 PRINT SPC(10) "BLUNDER! "
920 REM *** PAUSE FOR A MOMENT ***
930 FOR DE = 1 TO 400: NEXT
940 CLR
950 GOTO 90
960 REM ***********************
970 REM *** SPRITE MAKER ***
980 REM ***********************
990 FOR COUNT = 0 TO 62
1000 POKE 192 * 64 + COUNT,255
1010 NEXT COUNT
1020 POKE 2040,192:POKE 2041,192
1030 POKE 2042,192:POKE 2043,192
1040 REM *** SET WIDTH OF BOXES ***
1050 POKE 53271,15:POKE 53277,15
1060 REM *** SWITCH ON FOUR SPRITES ***
1070 POKE 53269,15
1080 REM *** BOXES HORIZONTAL "X" POSITIONS ***
1090 POKE 53248,50:POKE 53250,110:POKE 53252,170:POKE
57254,230
1100 REM *** BOXES VERTICAL "Y" POSITIONS ***
1110 POKE 53249,100:POKE 53251,100
1120 POKE 53253,100:POKE 53255,100
1130 REM *** PAINT SPRITES BLACK ***
1140 FOR COUNT = 53287 TO 53290
1150 POKE COUNT,0:NEXT
1160 POKE 54296,15
```

```
1170 RETURN
1180 REM ********************
1190 REM *** SET-UP VOICE ***
1200 REM ********************
1210 FOR ER = 54272 TO 54295:POKE ER,0:NEXT ER
1220 REM *** PULSE WIDTH ***
1230 POKE 54275,8
1240 POKE 54282,8
1250 POKE 54289,8
1260 REM *** ATTACK/DECAY
1270 POKE 54277,88
1280 POKE 54284,88
1290 POKE 54291,88
1300 REM *** WAVEFORM ***
1310 POKE 54276,17:POKE 54283,17:POKE 54290,17
1320 REM *** CHORDS ***
1330 POKE 54272;L1:POKE 54273,H1
1340 POKE 54279,L2:POKE 54280,H2
1350 POKE 54286,L3:POKE 54287,H3
1360 FOR DE = 1 TO SK:NEXT DE
1370 RETURN
```

19.

Bundesarchiv, Bild 102-10248
Foto: o. Ang. | August 1930

Car Ownership Cost

Are you considering buying another car? How much will it really cost to own per year, per month, and per mile? The costs will be of two types: fixed and variable. Fixed costs include yearly depreciation of the vehicle, the installment loan, interest, insurance, taxes, license plates, and municipal stickers. Variable costs include fuel, oil and grease, tires, batteries, windshield wipers, burnt-out headlights, tolls, and the Saturday afternoon wash'n'wax job.

Fixed costs are hard to allocate. For instance, if fixed charges total $1,000 a year, and the car is driven 24,000 miles that year, fixed costs total four cents a mile. But if you drive only 5,000 miles in a year, fixed costs jump to twenty cents a mile.

One thing is certain: the cost of owning and operating a well- maintained car goes down sharply as it gets older, especially after the first year. This is primarily due to a decrease in depreciation. The drop in fixed charges, however, is partially offset by an increase in maintenance costs. Nevertheless, for a compact car, the cost per mile falls from about 58 cents in its first year—including fixed and variable costs—to about 22 cents on its tenth birthday.

Much of the car's total cost over ten years depends on trade-in allowance for the old heap, actual price paid for the car, interest rate, and the depreciation schedule set up with the car's anticipated use.

Fuel cost is another important consideration in either buying a new car or selling an old one. If a particular model gets 24 MPG, and another gets 14 MPG, assuming fuel costs $1.25 a gallon, and each car is driven 10,000 miles, fuel will cost $296 less for the more fuel- efficient vehicle. Over a long period of time, that amounts to a size- able sum.

Standard transmissions normally get better gas mileage because the engine is not straining at a stop sign to move the car forward. A standard transmission idles, the engine with the transmission out of gear. However, poor driving habits can blow that advantage.

Axle ratios affect how many engine revolutions are needed to turn the wheel one full turn. Low axle ratios save gas and keep the engine running at a lower RPM. High ratios gear the engine down for pulling trailers or hauling "toppers" [top part of a camper).

Diesel engines can reward drivers with an increase in mileage of as much as 25 percent, but they are more expensive to purchase and maintain. One has to drive lots of miles to make the additional up-front expense payoff. Besides the monetary expense, one should consider the controversy over whether or not diesel engines emit cancer-causing pollutants.

Tires affect mileage. Low pressure increases road resistance, and thus gasoline consumption. Keep tires properly inflated. It's a good idea to invest in your own tire gauge, so you won't have to face those grumpy service station personnel who only begrudgingly hand over a filthy gauge and stare at you. Radial tires cost more initially, but deliver 3 to 8 percent better mileage. Plus, they last longer and improve handling.

Cruise control can eliminate a driver's inconsistency by keeping the car moving at a relatively constant velocity—without those inadvertent leg shifts.

Air conditioners use lots of engine horsepower, typically pulling down gas mileage 1-3 MPG. Is it worth it? Power seats, antennas, brakes, and steering also rob fuel dollars.

The biggest waste of fuel is an out of tune engine. A tune-up usually pays for itself in a few tankfuls.

How the Program Works

Line 90 blanks the screen.

Line 100 displays the program title.

Lines 130 through 410 ask for the fixed-cost particulars-how many MPG, cost of loan payments, and the like. The answers are stored in descriptive numeric variables.

Lines 450 and 470 perform preliminary calculations.

Line 520 tallies all of the fixed costs, storing the sum in the variable TA.

Lines 540 through 600 break down the cost per mile, per month, and per year.
Lines 630 through 750 format and print the results.

String and Numeric Variables

MI Average miles driven per year. MG Miles per gallon.

PG Cost per gallon of fuel.

LN Amount of monthly car payment (enter 0 if none).

IN Cost to insure vehicle for one year.

TU Money usually spent in a year on engine work.

SH A new set of shocks needed?

TR New tires needed? Snow tires?

LU Amount usually spent over a year on oil changes and grease jobs.

MS Amount spent on windshield wiper blades, burnt-out tail lights, and so on.

TA Total sum of expenses.

PM Cost per mile to operate car.

MN Average costs per month.

FP Fuel cost per year.

LN Annual loan payments.

GA Gallons fuel burned annually.

The Program

```
10 REM *********************
20 REM *
30 REM *
40 REM * CAR OWNERSHIP COST *
50 REM *
60 REM *
70 REM *********************
80 REM *** BLANK SCREEN ***
90 PRINT CHR$(147)
100 PRINT SPC(1) "CAR COST CALCULATOR"
110 PRINT
120 REM *** INPUT EACH COST VARIABLE ***
130 PRINT "MILES DRIVEN"
140 INPUT MI
150 PRINT
160 PRINT "MPG"
170 INPUT MG
180 PRINT
190 PRINT "PRICE PER GALLON"
200 INPUT PG
210 PRINT
220 PRINT "LOAN PAYMENT"
230 INPUT LN
240 PRINT
250 PRINT "INSURANCE (1 YR)"
260 INPUT IN
270 PRINT
280 PRINT "TUNE-UP"
290 INPUT TU
300 PRINT
310 PRINT "SHOCK ABSORBERS"
320 INPUT SH
330 PRINT
340 PRINT "NEW TIRES"
350 INPUT TR
360 PRINT
370 PRINT "OIL CHANGES & LUBE"
380 INPUT LU
```

```
390 PRINT
400 PRINT "MISC. EXPENSES"
410 INPUT MS
420 REM ******************************
430 REM *** CALCULATE TOTAL AMOUNT ***
440 REM ******************************
450 LN=LN*12: REM LOAN PAYMENTS (1 YR.)
460 REM *** GALLONS FUEL BURNED ANNUALLY ***
470 GA=MI/MG
480 REM *** FUEL COST ANNUALLY ***
490 FP = INT(((PG * GA) * 100) + .5)/100
500 TA= FP + LN + IN + TU + SH + TR + LU + MS
510 REM *** CONVERT TO TWO PLACE DECIMAL ***
520 TA= INT ((TA * 100) + 0.5)/100
530 REM *** FIGURE PER MILE COST ***
540 PM=TA/MI
550 REM *** CONVERT TO TWO DECIMAL ***
560 PM= INT ((PM * 100) + 0.5)/100
570 REM *** FIGURE MONTHLY OPERATING AMOUNT ***
580 MN=TA/12
590 REM *** CONVERT TO TWO PLACE DECIMAL ***
600 MN = INT((MN * 100) + .5)/100
 610 REM *** DISPLAY PROGRAM RESULTS ***
620 PRINT CHR$(147): REM *** CLEAR SCREEN ***
630 PRINT:PRINT
640 PRINT "ANNUAL OPERATING COST"
650 PRINT
660 PRINT
670 PRINT "PER MILE";"$";PM
680 PRINT
690 PRINT"COST PER MONTH ";"$";MN
700 PRINT
710 PRINT"FUEL (YEAR)";"$";FP
720 PRINT
730 PRINT "--------------------"
740 PRINT
750 PRINT "TOTAL";"$";TA
760 END
```

20.

Road Trip Cost Tabulator

Here's a simple way to plan a trip and know ahead of time how much money you'll need to enjoy the journey. Plug in the miles you'll drive, round trip. If there will be a lot of sightseeing once you get there, don't forget to tally in those extra miles. Does the engine burn oil? If so, you can calculate that additional cost.

Next, how many miles per gallon does the engine get? Remember, EPA ratings are only a general indication of how well, or poorly, a car will perform. That kind of information is best gathered over a couple of months with scrupulous record-keeping. Perhaps you'd like to design a simple program for encoding those results.

How much will fuel cost on the road? Truck stops and other fueling stations located on well-traveled highways tend to charge inflated prices. Gasoline may be a nickel or a dime per gallon cheaper in your neighborhood than somewhere on Interstate 80. Plan ahead.

If you are going to sleep in a motel and enjoy the conveniences of a real bed and a sauna, include the average price you'll be paying for a room. If you will camp out along the way, type in that fee.

How many days will you be away from home? How much will be budgeted for food per day?

With all variables entered, the screen will clear and display a breakdown of the trip. You'll know at a glance how much fuel and oil, lodging, and food will cost. Further breakdowns will include the total cost, cost per-mile and cost per-day.p;;;

How the Program Works

Line 170 blanks the screen. Typically this program consists of a prompt such as: ROUND TRIP MILES? Inputting the information stores it in a numeric variable. This is true of MPG, motel prices, and so on.

Later, in line 470, the calculation begins.

With all of the information entered, line 550 will figure out how much it will cost to drive the car from point A to point B.

Line 510 figures out how much it will cost to stay in a motel.

Line 530 figures out foodcost for the total number of days you'll be gone.

Line 550 totals all of the costs involved.

Line 590 breaks it down into a per-day figure.

Line 630 calculates the per-mile figure.

Line 640 blanks the screen.

Lines 660 through 800 format and display the cost breakdowns.

String and Numeric Variables

MI Round trip miles.

A$ - Yes or No. (Engine burns oil?)

MG Miles driven per gallon of fuel.

FU Cost of a gallon of fuel.

MO Anticipated cost for one night in motel room.

LO Number of nights to be spent in motel.

DA Total days away from home.

FO Cost of food per day.

TA Total amount needed for gas, oil, food, and motel.

MI Average per-mile cost.

OI Miles driven before quart of oil burned.

PR Cost of a quart of oil.

The Program

```
100 REM ***************************
110 REM *
120 REM *
130 REM *** TRIP COST TABULATOR ***
140 REM *
150 REM *
160 REM ***************************
170 PRINT CHR$(147)
180 PRINT
190 PRINT SPC(4) "TRIP EXPENSES"
200 PRINT
210 PRINT "ROUND TRIP MILES"
220 INPUT MI
230 PRINT
240 PRINT "CAR BURNS OIL (Y/N)"
250 GET A$:IF A$ = "" THEN 250
260 REM *** IF OIL BURNER GO TALLY AMOUNT ***
270 IF A$ = "Y" THEN GOSUB 850
280 PRINT 290 PRINT "MPG (HWY)"
300 INPUT MG
310 PRINT
```

90

```
320 PRINT"COST GALLON"
330 INPUT FU
340 PRINT
350 PRINT"COST FOR MOTEL"
360 INPUT MO
370 PRINT
380 PRINT"NIGHTS IN MOTEL"
390 INPUT LO
400 PRINT
410 PRINT"DAYS ON ROAD"
420 INPUT DA
430 PRINT
440 PRINT"FOOD BUDGET (DAY)"
450 INPUT FO
460 REM *** CALCULATE FUEL COST ***
470 FU = (MI/MG) * FU
480 REM *** CONVERT TO TWO PLACE DECIMAL ***
490 FU = INT((FU * 100) + .5) /100
500 REM *** CALCULATE LODGING COSTS ***
510 LO = LO * MO
520 REM *** CALCULATE FOOD EXPENSE ***
530 FO = FO * DA
540 REM *** TOTAL ***
550 TA = FO + LO + OI + FU
560 REM *** CONVERT TO TWO PLACE DECIMAL ***
570 TA = INT(( TA * 100) + .5) / 100
580 REM *** CALCULATE DAILY EXPENSE ***
590 DA = TA /DA
600 REM *** CONVERT TO TWO PLACE DECIMAL ***
610 DA = INT((DA * 100) + .5)/100
620 REM *** PER MILE COST ***
630 MI = (TA/MI)
640 PRINT CHR$(147)
650 REM *** DISPLAY RESULTS ***
660 PRINT "TRIP WILL COST: $";TA
670 PRINT
680 PRINT "GAS $";FU
690 PRINT
700 PRINT "OIL $";OI
710 PRINT
```

```
720 PRINT "LODGING $";LO
730 PRINT
740 PRINT "MEALS $";FO
750 PRINT
760 PRINT
770 PRINT "PER MILE $";MI
780 PRINT
790 PRINT
800 PRINT "PER DAY $";DA
810 END
820 REM ***********************
830 REM * CALCULATE OIL COSTS *
840 REM ***********************
850 PRINT
860 PRINT "MILES PER QUART"
870 INPUT OI
880 PRINT
890 PRINT "COST PER QUART"
900 INPUT PR
910 OI = MI/OI
920 OI = OI * PR
930 RETURN
```

21

Meal Planner

How much does it cost to cook that exotic quiche your significant lover craves? What about those expensive Austrian pastries (Gugelhupf Cake and Dobos Torte)you've been aching to try, but were troubled because they might be too expensive to create? Or, just maybe, you'd like to try your hand at the Stroganoff recipe that has been handed down in your family for generations.

No matter what the reason, or the recipe, it's time to get with the program that makes menu-planning easy. Just fill in the blanks. Fill in the number of ingredients you want to use, and, one by one, fill in the cost of each item.

They'll be totaled, and in an instant you'll be apprised of how much an individual serving costs, as well as the total cost of preparing the meal. It's as easy as saying, "*Bon appetit!*"

How the Program Works

Line 170 blanks the screen.
Line 210 gets the number of ingredients in the recipe.
Line 280 will loop back once for each one of those ingredients.
Line 250 asks for the cost of each ingredient and assigns cost to the variable IT.
Line 270 adds each ingredient to the sum of PR.

Line 280 keeps the loop going until each ingredient cost is entered.

Line 300 asks for the number of people to be served.

Line 310 calculates how much it will cost to feed each person

Lines 350 through 380 display how much the total meal cost is, as well as the cost per individual serving.

String and Numeric Variables

NU Number of ingredients in recipe.

CO Current place in loop.

IT Cost of ingredient.

SE How many to be served this culinary masterpiece you are slaving over, and finally, cost per serving.

PR Total cost of meal.

The Program

```
100 REM ***************
110 REM *
120 REM *
130 REM * MEAL PLANNER *
140 REM *
150 REM *
160 REM ***************
170 PRINT CHR$(147)
180 PRINT:PRINT
190 PRINT "MEAL PLANNER"
200 PRINT:PRINT
210 INPUT "INGREDS. IN RECIPE ";NU
220 REM *** COME BACK FOR EACH INGRED. ***
230 FOR CO = 1 TO NU
240 PRINT
250 PRINT "COST OF INGRED. #";CO;:INPUT IT
260 REM *** TALLY COSTS ***
270 PR = PR + IT
280 NEXT CO
290 PRINT
300 INPUT "NUMBER OF GUESTS ";SE
310 SE = PR/SE
320 REM *****************************
330 REM *** DISPLAY PROGRAM RESULTS ***
340 REM *****************************
350 PRINT
360 PRINT "TOTAL COST OF MEAL = $";PR
370 PRINT
380 PRINT "COST PER SERVING = $";SE
390 END
```

22.
Utility Audit

Have you ever wondered how expensive it is to run the microwave oven for an hour? Or, how about a house full of lights that no one is using? It's an eye-opener to discover that 240 watts worth of light bulbs at 7.5 cents per kWh cost about $4.80 a month, or over $50 a year! Walking family members through this home energy audit can help convince them they really ought to switch off lights in rooms when they leave, or during winter months, don a warm sweater over that summer T-shirt.

What about the argument that it costs more to switch a lamp off then on again an hour later than simply to let it burn? While that might have been true in the old days when sloppy wall switches let current arc across poor contacts, these days it's simply not true. Turn off lights in empty rooms and save cash.

By the way, it's interesting to note the power supply on the Commodore 64 is rated at about 20 watts. Monitors and televisions usually are rated between 100 and 500 watts. (Tube sets pull more current than transistorized versions).How much does it cost to run a computer for an hour?

To find out, RUN the program. You'll need to know how much you are paying for electricity. Most utility bills list the rate per kilowatt-hour (kWh). Plug in the figure when the program asks for it. (Note: enter 7.5 cents as .075.)

Next, plug in the rating, in watts, of the Commodore 64 or any other appliance you wish to calculate. After some quick computations, the program will show how much it costs to run that appliance for as many hours as you asked it totally. Additionally, you'll find out what that cost translates into for a day and for a month.

One last note. A computer doesn't think of ten and a half cents (per kWh) as 10.5. Instead, it sees it as .105.

How the Program Works

Line 180 blanks the screen.

Line 220 asks for and inputs the cost of electricity in your town. We will save this value in KW and use it as many times as you want to figure different watts (WT) and hours (HO) used per day. More on this in a moment.

Line 240 inputs the Watts burned by whatever appliance you are scrutinizing.

Line 260 inputs how many hours a day this appliance typically hums away at its assigned task.

Line 270 is the workhorse of this program. It computes how much of a kilowatt-hour you are using. Line 290 converts this figure to a two-place decimal for a neater-looking display.

Lines 320 through 410 format and display how much it costs to run he appliance by the hour, day, and month.

Line 440 routes the program back to line 230. This way, if you want to plug in the watts rating of a different appliance, or different running time, you can do so without having to start all over again.

String and Numeric Variables

KW Cost per kilowatt-hour (KWH).

WT How many watts used by appliance.

HO Hours used per day.

PR Cost per hour to use appliance.

DY Daily cost based on HO per day.

MU Monthly cost based on HO times DY.

The Program

```
100 REM ****************** ***
110 REM *
120 REM *
130 REM * UTILITY AUDIT
140 REM *
150 REM *
160 REM ***********************
170 REM *** BLANK SCREEN ***
180 PRINT CHR$(147)
190 PRINT SPC(1)"UTILITY BILL MONITOR"
200 REM *** COST OF KWH ***
210 PRINT
220 PRINT "RATE PER KWH";:INPUT KW
230 PRINT
240 PRINT "WATT RATING";:INPUT WT
250 PRINT
260 PRINT "HOURS USED DAILY";:INPUT HO
270 PR=(WT/1000)*KW
280 REM *** COMPUTE TO TWO PLACE DECIMAL ***
290 PR=INT((PR*190)+0.5)/100
300 PRINT
310 REM *** DISPLAY HOURLY RATE ***
320 PRINT "COSTS$";PR;"HOUR"
330 DY=PR*HO
340 REM *** COMPUTE MONTHLY AMOUNT ***
350 MU=DY * 30
360 PRINT
370 REM *** DAILY AMOUNT ***
380 PRINT "$";DY;"PER DAY"
390 PRINT
400 REM *** MONTHLY AMOUNT ****
410 PRINT "$";MU;"MONTH"
420 REM *** WANT TO DO FURTHER ANALYSIS ***
430 GET KE$:IF KE$ = "" THEN 430
440 GOTO 230
```

23.

Heat Loss Cost Analysis

It has been one of those days. Outdoors it's ten degrees below zero, and a waist-high snowdrift blocks the path to the Detroit-built Belchfire 88 that probably won't start anyway. But somehow, through all the wind and blowing snow, the mail person delivers the utility bill. Slowly, you open the envelope and read the bad news.

If you want to do something about it, you can. The heat loss program will calculate about how many BTUs slip out through the living room picture window, any other window, or even the old wooden door in the back of the house. Kick in a few other bits of information, and you can tally how much money is lost through poor insulation.

Armed with that kind of data, a homeowner can plug in different heat-saving factors, like installing storm windows, drapes, and a new steel door. The program will indicate how much money you could save by upgrading the house's insulation. Match those savings against the cost of installing the energy conservation items, and you can determine whether or not it would pay to do the work. Most often, it pays off big.

Begin the program by plugging in the efficiency rating of the heat source. It can be any kind of gas or fuel oil furnace, electric baseboard heater, wood stove, or kerosene heater. This efficiency rating is an important figure. It tells how well the unit exchanges its energy for usable heat. For instance, some fuel oil furnaces are rated at 50 percent, and some kerosene heaters are rated at 99 per- cent efficient.

The next consideration is the BTU value of the fuel. In other words, for each unit expended, be it kilowatt-hour, cord of firewood, or gallon of fuel oil, how many BTUs will it generate?

See Table 23-1, immediately below, to get the appropriate figure.

Table 23-1	
FUEL	**HEAT VALUES**
Electricity	3,412 BTUs per kWh
Fuel Oil	138,000 BTUs per gallon
Natural Gas	100,000 BTUs per therm
L. P. Gas	93,000 BTUs per gallon
Firewood (hardwood)	24,000,000 BTUs per cord
Firewood (soft)	15,000,000 BTUs per cord

You'll need to know also how much the unit of energy costs. Enter it as decimal information. For instance, 71/2 cents per kWh is .075. $1.30 per gallon would be entered as 1.3, and so on.

Since we are figuring heat loss per year, we need to know how many hours the heat source will be operational per average winter. Each city has a different climate, and thanks to the United States weather service, there is a handy number we can plug in. It's called degree heating hours (DHH), and Table 23-2 has a representative number of cities. Check for the city nearest your climatic conditions.

Now to the house. Consider one area at a time. Say we want to know how much heat is lost through a window five feet tall by seven feet wide. Enter each dimension at the prompt. The program will take care of the multiplication needed to get the area in square feet.

Next we need to know the R-value, or the area's resistance to heat loss. See Table 23-3. With that final number plugged in, the program will print out:

1.   How many BTUs are lost through that surface.
2.   How much that loss costs per season.

That information can be shocking. A 5 x 7 foot single-pane window (R1) in a Boston home burning fuel oil with a 60-percent efficient furnace loses 4,725,000 BTUs. All those BTUs, by the way, cost $74 a season.

By adding a storm window and thermal drape, the R-value of the same 5 x 7 foot window is increased from 1 to 2.1. Heat loss drops to 2,249,999 BTUs. Those BTUs, by comparison, cost only $35, or $39 less per year.

To aid in considering insulation upgrades, the program has a built-in feature. After each calculation, the cursor automatically returns to the R-value input line. Plug in a new R-value, and the new heat loss and dollar figure comes up on screen. It's an easy way to assess whether or not it pays to insulate.

Table 23-3	
Material	**R VALUES**
Single glass with shade	1.0
Single glass with lined drape	1.3
Double glass or, a storm window	1.8
Double glass with drape	2.1
Triple glass 2.8	2.8
Double glass with shutter	9.6
Wooden door	1.56
Insulated steel door	1.69
Wood siding	.81
Fiberglas insulation (3.5")	11.0
Wall with 3½ inches. Fiberglas insulation	13.0
Wall with 6-inches. Fiberglas insulation	22.5

How the Program Works

Line 80 blanks the screen.

Line 100 specifies black characters to be displayed.

Line 160 asks for and inputs the rated efficiency of the heat source. This percentage is stored in the variable EF.

Line 180 converts EF to an integer.

Line 210 inputs the BTU value of the fuel.

Line 240 gets the cost of the fuel, be it per gallon, cord, KWH, or whatever.

Line 260 calculates how much heat is lost due to design of the furnace. Line 280 tabulates that cost per million BTUs.

Line 290 converts cost to a two-place decimal for a nicer-looking display.

Line 320 inputs how many hours (DHH) per year the furnace typically will need to run.

Lines 350 through 390 figure the cubic foot area of the window, or door, to be studied.

Line 440 figures heat loss, a formula is based on area, degree heating hours (DH), and the R-value heating hours (DH), and the R-value.

Lines 480 and 490 display the annual heat loss in black characters.

Line 510 converts the loss to a million units.

Lines 520 and 530 translate that loss into dollars.

Lines 530 and 540 compute how much money heat loss costs per winter.

Line 550 displays that loss in dollars.

Line 580 sends us back to try new R-values to see how increasing the R-value helps.

Table 23-2	
Locale	DEGREE HEATING HOURS
Anchorage, AK	261000
Flagstaff, AZ	172000
Denver, CO	151000
Hartford, CT	148000
Wilmington, DE	118000
Boise, ID	139000
Boston, MA	135000
Duluth, MN	240000
Buffalo, NY	168000
New York, NY	115000
Portland, OR	111000
Austin, TX	47520
Seattle, WA	106000

String and Numeric Variables

EF Tells how efficiently the heat source uses its fuel.

HE Number of BTUs yielded by one unit of the fuel.

PR Cost of one unit of fuel.

DH Degree heating hours. Number of hours heat source typically will run in winter.

WI Width of area to be studied.

HT Height of area to be studied.

AR Surface area.

R R-Value.

LO BTU (heat) lost through area being studied.

DO How many dollars the heat loss costs per year.

The Program

```
10 REM ************************
20 REM *
30 REM *
40 REM * HEATING LOSS ANALYSIS *
50 REM *
60 REM *
70 REM ************************
80 PRINT CHR$(147)
90 REM *** BLACK CHARS. ***
100 PRINT CHR$(144)
110 PRINT
120 PRINT "HEATING BILL ANALYSIS
130 REM *** HOW EFFICIENT IS HEAT SOURCE ***
140 PRINT CHR$(5)
150 PRINT
160 PRINT "EFFICIENCY IN %";;INPUT EF
170 REM *** CONVERT TO DECIMAL ***
180 EF=EF/100
190 PRINT
200 REM *** FUEL YIELDS HOW MANY BTUS PER UNIT ***
210 PRINT "BTU VALUE":;INPUT HE
220 REM *** COST PER GALLON, KWH, ETC ***
230 PRINT
240 PRINT "COST PER UNIT ";:INPUT PR
250 REM *** FIGURE COST PER MILLION BTU ***
260 HE = EF * HE
270 PR = PR/HE
280 PR = PR * 1000000
290 PR = INT((PR*100) +.5)/100
300 PRINT
310 REM *** GET WEATHER SERVICE INFORMATION ***
320 PRINT "DEG HEAT HRS";:INPUT DH
330 PRINT
340 REM *** GET AREA TO STUDY ***
350 PRINT "WIDTH";:INPUT WI
360 PRINT
370 PRINT "HEIGHT";:INPUT HT
```

```
380 REM *** FIGURE AREA OF WINDOW ***
390 AR = WI * HT
400 PRINT
410 REM *** GET NEW R-VALUE ***
420 PRINT "R-VALUE";:INPUT R
430 REM *** FIGURE HEAT LOSS ***
440 LO = AR * DH * (1/R)
450 REM *** CONVERT TO DECIMAL ***
460 LO = INT((LO * 100)+.5)/100
470 PRINT
480 PRINT CHR$(144)
490 PRINT "HEAT LOSS";LO;"BTU"
500 REM *** CONVERT TO MILLION ***
510 LO = L0/1000000
520 REM *** FIGURE MONEY LOST PER WINTER ***
530 DO = LO*PR
540 DO = INT ((DO*100)+0.5)/100
550 PRINT: PRINT "COSTS YOU $";DO
560 REM *** TRY ANOTHER R-VALUE ***
570 GET KE$: IF VE$ = "" THEN 570
580 GOTO 80
```

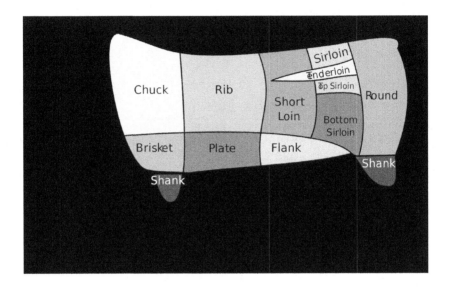

24

Bulk Purchase Tabulator

Quantity purchases can substantially reduce your food bill. Meat markets, for example, usually sell large cuts at a lower price per pound than the individually wrapped cuts that line the meat case. Those consumer-sized packages are a convenience for which you've been paying extra. Learning a few of the ins and outs of purchasing meat in quantities will save you big money.

"Let the buyer beware" is the watchword. Some unscrupulous meat dealers are ‧ noted for butchering the beef and taking out two or three T-bone steaks. Always ask for the fat and bones. It lets the meat cutter know you're not an amateur. He or she will know you expect an accounting for every pound of beef you've paid for. In truth, the butcher could still lift a couple of rib-eyes, substitute another customer's bones, and you'd never know. But the idea is to come across with a little more savvy than the average person.

Bait-and-switch is another trick to watch out for. Say you've spent months learning how to tell the kind of marbling that insures a tender portion. You pick out what looks like a good cut, and that's the last you ever see of it as it's wheeled into the back room for processing. Months later, you shake your head and wonder how a selection that looked so tender could be so tough. What happened? Well, you did see a good portion, which ten other people probably picked for their own that day. And you ended up with an entirely different piece of meat. Because of this bait-and-switch practice, some zealous customers demand to watch the carving-up practice.

Don't be surprised when a full 30- to 40-percent of the original weight disappears into the heap of bones and fat. That's standard, and you'll pay for the waste at the same per-pound cost as the ribs,roast, and steaks. Remember, you are buying the entire portion, not just the good parts.

Perhaps you'd like to try your hand at cutting the meat yourself. If you're interested, the Government Printing Office puts out some very informative literature, amounting to a free crash-course in butchering meat. Ask for pamphlet AFS 6-4 entitled "How to Save Money with Large Cuts of Meat."

No matter who does the bloody work, storage is an important factor for a quarter of a ton of beef. How will you store it: in the top compartment of the refrigerator-freezer, a commercial locker, or a home freezer? For purposes of calculation, consider that one cubic foot of freezer space will store about thirty-five pounds of wrapped meat. If the shapes of the cuts are irregular, figure on fewer pounds per cubic foot.

Wrapping technique is most important. Moisture loss is bad for meat and tends to occur with exposure to air. To prevent it, use heavy aluminum foil, heavily waxed freezer paper, or laminated paper. Plastic bags will work well if double-bagged, twisted shut, doubled back on the twist, and then sealed with wire ties.

When two or more steaks are wrapped in the same pack, slide a couple sheets of waxed paper in between the two to prevent them from freezing together. Once the individual cuts are wrapped, mark the contents and the day's date.

How long will frozen meats stay good? That depends on the temperature. The colder the temperature, the longer meat will keep. At zero degrees, steaks and roasts can keep from eight months to a year. Ground beef and lamb are good for about four months; while ground pork keeps from one to three months.

While this program helps figure the cost effectiveness of buying a quarter or side of beef, it could easily be modified to consider bushels of tomatoes, a peck of potatoes, or even big bunches of carrots for canning.

Since the program is written for meat, tell the computer how many pounds you bought, at what price per pound, how much the butchering fee was, and, finally, how many pounds were left after processing.

After the last entry, the program will tell how much you paid for the total package, and how much per pound it effectively cost.

How the Program Works

Line 170 blanks the screen.

Line 220 inputs the pounds of whatever food is being considered. Maybe it's carrots or cabbage about to be canned.

Line 250 calculates how much it costs to buy that food.

Line 270 inputs the processing charge. For meat, it means butchering. For carrots on their way to be canned, processing includes salt and mason jars.

Line 290 considers the reality that not all the food is usable. There is always waste. After processing, how many pounds are left?

Line 320 adds the original purchase price to the cost of any processing or supplies.

Line 330 figures out the cost per pound; while line 350 converts the figure to a two-place decimal.

Lines 390 through 420 display the results.

String and Numeric Variables

BE Pounds of food bought.

PO Price per pound.

FE Cost of butchering, canning, and so on.

LE Amount of food left after any waste is subtracted.

PR The sum of food purchase, plus processing and supplies.

PP Ultimate purchase price per pound to make this bulk purchase.

The Program

```
100 REM ****************************
110 REM *
120 REM *
130 REM * BULK PURCHASE TABULATOR *
140 REM *
150 REM *
1150 REM ****************************
170 PRINT CHR$.(147): REM CLEAR SCREEN
180 PRINT
190 PRINT "BULK PURCHASE"
200 PRINT:PRINT
210 REM *** COST VARIABLES ***
220 PRINT "POUNDS";:INPUT BE
230 PRINT
240 PRINT "$ PER POUND";:INPUT PO
250 PR = BE * PO
260 PRINT
270 PRINT "PROCESSING CHARGE";:INPUT FE
280 PRINT
290 PRINT "POUNDS LEFT"
300 INPUT LE
310 REM *** CALCULATE COSTS ***
320 PR = PR + FE
330 PP = (PR/LE)
340 REM *** CONVERT TO TWO PLACE DECIMAL ***
350 PP = INT((PP*100)+ .5)/100
360 REM *****************************
370 REM *** DISPLAY PROGRAM RESULTS ***
380 REM *****************************
390 PRINT " -----------------"
400 PRINT "TOTAL","$";PR
410 PRINT:PRINT
420 PRINT "AVERAGE","$": PP
```

25.

Smart Typewriter/Dumb Word Processor

A word processor doesn't have to be loaded with frills to be valuable, as long as you don't expect right-margin justification, pagination, and all the fancy extras that come with a commercial piece of software. Without the frills, this program will perform almost all of your text-writing needs. Write letters, poetry, a best-selling novel, whatever you'd like. In fact, most of this book was written with this program. Here's how to use it.

Type in the program, SAVE it, then RUN. The menu displays three choices. Just press 1, 2, or 3 and hit RETURN. If your choice was I, the screen will blank and ask for the name of the file under which you want to save your work.

Back to the filename selection. Once you enter one, the screen will blank and a prompt will tell you it's okay to start typing. If you make a mistake, use the backspace key to correct it.

Each line of text can hold up to 88 characters. This is important. Once you have typed a line and hit RETURN, it can't be changed. It is as good as written in stone (silicon?). You can't correct it. Be careful of hitting the RUN/STOP key. The logic being that the last thing your sunny disposition needs is to hit the break key in the middle of com- posing an important letter!

When you finish drafting the document and are ready to quit, hit RETURN at the beginning of the line. It must be the first, and only, character of the line. With this, the write-text program ends, and control returns to the task menu. Remember, the only way to quit is by hitting RETURN.

So now we're back at the menu. Choose 1, 2, or 3. Let's say that you've typed a 2 because you'd like to read over a letter you've written to your Congressman regarding an issue very sensitive to you. First, rewind to the beginning of the tape where the text is stored, then press the play button. The screen will clear and ask for the filename of the all-important document.

This is a good time to talk about choice of filenames. Sometimes it's hard to remember how a document was filed. It helps to have a system. For instance, label all correspondence with the last name of the recipient, followed by an filename extender labeling it as a letter. One example might be KENNEDY.LET. A speech, on the other hand, might be labeled: WHALES.TXT. It's not terribly important which system you use, as long as it works.

Once you've told the Commodore 64 which file you want to call up, the screen will clear and display said file's first twenty lines. Then it stops. To see twenty more lines, tap any key, except break. Once we've read the last line of the file, a little message will let us know. Again, hit any key to go on. After having read the length of the file, control will loop back to the task menu. If you've finished work, type a 3 and the program will end.

How the Program Works

Line 190 blanks the screen.

Lines 210 through 300 display the task menu.

Lines 310 through 340 return the user's choice and send the program off to do its chosen task. If the user has typed any number other than a 1, 2, or 3, the program automatically progresses to "WRITE DOCUMENT".

Line 410 assigns the filename where the work will be stored.

Line 440 opens the file.

Line 480 zeroes the character count.

Line 510 reads each character as you type it.

Line 540 looks for a carriage return. If it's the first character in the line, it means you've finished work.

Line 590 stores each character typed in a numeric variable.

Line 600 checks for a carriage return at the end of a line. When encountered, it's off to line 630.

Lines 630 through 660 take each character saved and write them to the file, one at a time.

Line 670 goes to get the next line of text.

Line 690 closes the file.

Line 710 sends us back to the task menu.

Lines 750 through 770 display the prompts that ask which file you want to call up.

Line 790 opens that file.

Notice line 800. If you have a printer, enter this line with the REM. You'll also need the CMD statement. The line would look like this:

111

```
800 OPEN 2.4:CMD4
```

Line 830 reads one character of text at a time. Line 870 stops the display every time for you to press the space bar.

Line 880 tells the computer to look for the end of the file. When it reads that far, then close the file and go to line 950 where we'll close the file.

Lines 1040 and 1050 are the finished routine.

String and Numeric Variables

F1$ The cassette or disk file to be opened.

LI$ Read keyboard. Space bar pressed to halt display?

KE Which key pressed?

CO Number of characters read and displayed from file.

ST Status of file; read to end yet?

X Characters written to file.

```
100 REM *********************
110 REM *
120 REM *
130 REM ** SMART TYPEWRITER **
140 REM *
150 REM * DUMB WP
160 REM *
170 REM *********************
180 DIM FI$(14),KE(512)
190 PRINT CHR$(147)
200 REM *** REM DISPLAY MENU ***
210 PRINT
220 PRINT SPC(3)"W.P. TASK CHART"
230 PRINT
240 PRINT "1. WRITE DOCUMENT"
250 PRINT
260 PRINT "2. READ DOCUMENT"
270 PRINT
280 PRINT "3. DONE"
290 PRINT
300 PRINT SPC(3)"CHOOSE 1-3"
310 GET KE$: IF KE$ = "" THEN 310
320 PRINT CHR$(147)
330 KE = ASC(KE$)
340 ON KE-48 GOTO 360,750,1040
350 REM *** BLACK LETTERS ***
360 PRINT CHR$(144)
370 PRINT SPC(4)"WRITE DOCUMENT"
380 PRINT:PRINT
390 REM *** WHITE LETTERS ***
400 PRINT CHR$(5)
410 PRINT"NAMED:";:INPUT F1$
420 PRINT
430 PRINT SPC(5)"PLEASE WAIT"
440 OPEN 1,1,1,F1$
450 PRINT CHR$(147)
460 PRINT SPC(1)"PLEASE BEGIN TYPING"
470 PRINT
```

```
480 CO = 0
490 REM *** 1 CHARACTER AT A TIME ***
500 CO = CO + 1
510 GET KE$: IF KE$= "" THEN 510
520 KE = ASC(KE$): PRINT CHR$(KE);
530 REM *** DONE TYPING ***
540 IF CO = 1 AND KE = 13 THEN 690
550 REM *** BACKSPACE? ***
560 IF KE = 20 THEN CO = CO - 2:GOTO 500
570 IF CO < 1 THEN CO = 1
580 REM *** STORE TYPED CHARACTER ***
590 LET KE(CO) = KE
600 IF KE = 13 THEN 630
610 GOTO 500
620 REM ** WRITE TO FILE **
630 FOR X = 1 TO CO
640 KE = KE(X)
650 PRINT#1,CHR$(KE);
660 NEXT X
670 GOTO 480
680 REM **** CLOSE TEXT FILE ****
690 CLOSE 1
700 REM *** RETURN TO MENU ***
710 GOTO 190
720 REM *********************
730 REM *** READ TEXT FILE ***
740 REM *********************
750 PRINT SPC(4)"READ DOCUMENT"
760 CO = 0:PRINT
770 PRINT "NAMED";:INPUT F1$
780 REM *** OPEN TEXT FILE FOR READ ***
790 OPEN 1,1,0,F1$
800 REM *** OPEN #2,4 *** (PRINTER)
810 PRINT CHR$(147)
820 REM *** READ A CHAR. ***
830 GET #1,KE$
840 CO = CO + 1
850 REM *** DISPLAY A CHAR. ***
860 PRINT KES;
870 GET LI$: IF LI$ = CHR$(32) THEN 900
```

```
880 IF ST <> 64 THEN 830
890 GOTO 950
900 LI$ = "": GET LIS: IF LI$ = CHR$(32) THEN 830
910 GOTO 900
920 REM *******************
930 REM *** END OF FILE ***
940 REM *******************
950 CLOSE 1
960 PRINT:PRINT
970 PRINT SPC(5)"END OF FILE"
980 REM *** WAIT FOR KEY PRESS ***
990 GET KES: IF KE$ = "" THEN 990
1000 GOTO 190
1010 REM **********
1020 REM ** DONE **
1030 REM **********
1040 PRINT SPC(6) "GOOD BYE!"
1050 END
```

26

Carpool Worksheet

It's no surprise that carpooling saves money, whether it's a daily trip from the suburbs into work, or a group of friends sharing the expenses on a special trip. Regardless of the motivation, this program makes divvying up the costs a more pleasant task. This is a very uncomplicated system. Simply plug in the round-trip miles, the mileage of the vehicle you'll be traveling in, along with the cost per gallon of fuel, how many folks are going, plus any bridge or tollway fares you may be paying. That done, the results pop out. Perhaps you didn't like the results—too expensive. Okay, leave the big factory Lincoln in Ralph's driveway and take Mary's little red Chrysler. See how much difference the mileage makes.

How the Program Works

Line 150 blanks the screen.

Lines 160 through 310 format the dis-play that asks for all the particulars, such as mileage, miles driven, cost of fuel, and so on.

Lines 330 through 410 calculate the costs.

Notice lines 390, 400, and 410. They factor each of their variables down to a two-place decimal. That prevents a messy answer like:

COST PER MILE = .04567891234

Lines 430 through 470 display the calculations.

Line 500 sends us back to get new data; that is, if you're interested in com-paring different vehicles and their mileage.

String and Numeric Variables

MI Miles (round trip) to be driven.

MG Mileage per gallon.

FU Cost of gas or diesel fuel.

NU Passengers sharing expenses.

BR Total amount of bridge and highway fares.

PE Cost per round-trip mile.

RI Cost for each passenger's ride.

TR Total cost of trip.

The Program

```
100 REM ***********************
110 REM *
120 REM * CARPOOL WORKSHEET *
130 REM *
140 REM ***********************
150 PRINT CHR$(147): REM *** BLANK THE SCREEN ***
160 PRINT
170 PRINT "CAR POOL EXPENSE SHEET "
180 REM *** DETAIL THE EXPENSES ***
190 PRINT
200 PRINT "ROUND-TRIP MILES";:INPUT MI
210 PRINT
220 PRINT"MPG HWY";;INPUT MG
230 PRINT
240 PRINT"COST PER GAL.";:INPUT FU
250 PRINT
260 PRINT "RIDERS";:INPUT NU
270 PRINT
280 PRINT "FARES";;INPUT BR
290 PRINT
300 PRINT " ---------"
310 PRINT
320 REM *** CALCULATE COSTS ***
```

```
330 GA = MI/MG
340 FU = GA * FUEL
350 TR = BR + FU
360 PE = TR/MI
370 RI = TR/NU
380 REM *** CONVERT TO TWO DECIMAL PLACE ***
390 PE=INT ((PE*100)+0.5)/100
400 RI=INT ((RI*100)+0.5)/100
410 TR=INT ((TR*100)+0.5)/100
420 REM *** DISPLAY THE TABULATIONS ***
430 PRINT PER MILE=$";PE
440 PRINT
450 PRINT "PER RIDER $";RI
460 PRINT
470 PRINT "FOR TRIP SS$";TR
480 REM *** FIGURE WITH NEW VARIABLES ***
490 GET KE$:IF KE$ = "" THEN 490
500 GOTO 150
```

27

Music Composer

The Commodore 64 is a maestro when it comes to making music. With this composer, one can easily mimic a synthesizer key-board boasting three octaves with low C, middle C, and high C. More-over, each octave has its own voice. In this case, it means that the last note played, within its respective octave, will echo until a new note in that octave is played.

With the Music Composer program up and running, one by one press keys A through K. This plays middle C, from do to do. Likewise, play the notes Q through I to get a feel for high C.

Similarly, you can use the Z through comma keys to play the low C octave. Improvise your own tunes; let your imagination be your guide. Perhaps you will be delivered to a Gothic cathedral, a cobwebbed castle, or a rock concert sound stage.

How the Program Works

Line 170 blanks the screen.
Line 180 turns the voice chip's volume up to maximum.
Line 190 displays the program's logo.
Line 200 gets each key's number as you press it.
Lines 270 through 560 convert that number to represent a musical note.
Lines 580 through 660 play those notes.
Line 630 can be modified for an interesting variation. Change it to read:

```
630 POKE 54276,33
```

or,

```
POKE 54276,129
```

String and Numeric Variables

KE$(KE) Key pressed.
CO Blanks voice chip registers.
LOW/HI Loads musical note into the computer.

The Program

```
100 REM ******************
110 REM *
120 REM *
130 REM * MUSIC COMPOSER
140 REM *
150 REM *
160 REM ******************
170 PRINT CHR$(147)
180 POKE 54296,15
190 PRINT SPC(10) "MUSIC COMPOSER"
200 GET KE$: IF KE$ = "" THEN GOTO 200
210 REM * TRANSLATE TO ASCII *
220 KE = ASC(KE$)
230 REM *** DEFINE NOTES ****
240 REM ********************
250 REM * Z - , ARE LOW C **
260 REM ********************
270 IF KE = 90 THEN LOW = 134: HI = 37
280 IF KE = 88 THEN LOW = 161 :HI = 37
290 IF KE = 67 THEN LOW = 60: HI = 42
300 IF KE = 86 THEN LOW = 191: HI = 44
310 IF PE = 66 THEN LOW = 58: HI = 50
320 IF KE = 78 THEN LOW = 97: HI = 56
330 IF KE = 77 THEN LOW = 72: HI = 63
340 IF KE = 44 THEN LOW = 12: HI = 67
350 REM *****************
360 REM * A - K ARE MID C **
370 REM ********************
380 IF KE = 65 THEN LOW = 12: HI = 67
390 IF KE = 83 THEN LOW = 66: HI = 75
400 IF KE = 68 THEN LOW = 121: HI = 84
410 IF KE = 70 THEN LOW = 127: HI = 89
420 IF KE = 71 THEN LOW = 117: HI = 100
430 IF KE = 72 THEN LOW = 194: HI = 112
440 IF KE = 74 THEN LOW = 145: HI = 126
450 IF KE = 75 THEN LOW = 24: HI = 134
460 REM *********************
470 REM * Q TO I ARE HI C **
```

```
480 REM *********************
490 IF KE = 81 THEN LOW = 24: HI = 134
500 IF KE = 87 THEN LOW = 132: HI = 150
510 IF KE = 69 THEN LOW = 242: HI = 168
520 IF KE = 82 THEN LOW = 254: HI = 178
530 IF KE = 84 THEN LOW = 234: HI = 200
540 IF KE = 89 THEN LOW = 132: HI = 225
550 IF KE = 85 THEN LOW = 34: HI = 253
560 IF KE = 73 THEN LOW = 10:HI = 200
570 REM *** BLANK VOICE REGISTERS ***
580 FOR CO = 54272 TO 54295:POKE CO, 0: NEXT CO
590 REM * SET ATTACK/DECAY & SUSTAIN/RELEASE *
600 POKE 54277,88:POKE 54278,0
610 REM *** SET PULSE WIDTH ***
620 POKE 54275,8:POKE 54274,0
630 POKE 54276,17
640 REM *** LOAD NOTE ***
650 POKE 54272,LOW
660 POKE 54273,HI
670 REM *** NEXT NOTE ***
680 GOTO 200
```

28.
Typing Tutor

If you use a personal computer, efficient typing is a must to avoid the frustration of long hours at the keyboard, hunting and pecking, writing and correcting. If you understand the principles of touch typing, you are ahead of the game.

Briefly, the system requires you to look at the CRT or TV screen; it's forbidden to look at the keys. This is where the speed comes in. Train the mind so that the fingers instinctively know where the A, G, or L is located. If the mind and eye committee isn't slowed down by the hunt-and-peck variety of typing, it will be able to move through its creative tasks much more quickly. This takes practice.

The typing tutor provides an interesting way to attain that practice and test yourself. RUN the program and see the single character displayed in the center of the screen. Your job is to simply type each one as it comes up. If you respond correctly, a new one is displayed. However, if you hit the wrong key, a blunder sound resonates from the TV speaker.

Never fear, there are no penalties for being wrong; after all, you'll do better next time. After a few workouts with the tutor, word processing can become much less tedious, and programming will likewise be much less frustrating. When hard at it, remember to keep your eyes on the screen, and let your fingers do the typing.

How the Program Works

Line 120 blanks the screen.
Line 140 is the program's heart and soul. It generates a random number between 1 and 26. Each number corresponds to a letter in the alphabet, from A to Z (uppercase).
Line 160 adds 65 to each one of those numbers to convert it to ASCII, or the set of numbers the computer understands, for each A, B, C, or D.
Line 180 displays the letter you're being tested on.
Line 200 gets your response.
Line 250 compares your response with the correct answer. If you make a mistake, you'll hear about it.
Line 270 goes back to the well to test you on another character.
Lines 290 through 340 jump into action whenever you hit the wrong letter, by flashing the border red for an instant.
Line 300 determines just how long that instant will be. Line 310 paints the border its original color.

String and Numeric Variables

TY A random number representing a letter from A to Z.
KE$(KE) The letter you typed.
DE Delay loop counter.

The Program

```
10 REM *********************
20 REM *
30 REM *
40 REM * QWERT YUIOP *
50 REM *
60 REM * THE
70 REM *
80 REM * TYPING TUTOR
90 REM *
100 REM *
110 REM *********************
120 PRINT CHR$(147)
130 REM * GET RANDOM NUMBER BETWEEN 1 AND 26 *
140 TY=INT (26*RND(1))
150 REM * CONVERT RANDOM N0 TO LETTER IN ALPHABET *
160 TY=TY + 65
170 REM *** DISPLAY TEST LETTER ***
180 PRINT CHR$(TYPE);
190 REM *** GET LETTER STUDENT TYPES ***
200 GET KE$: IF KE$="" THEN 200
210 REM *** CONVERT KE$ TO ASCII NUMBER ***
220 KE=ASC(KE$)
230 REM * COMPARE STUDENTS LETTER TO TEST LETTER *
240 REM * IF WRONG LETTER FLASH BORDER RED *
250 IF KE <> TY THEN GOTO 290
260 REM *** TEST ANOTHER LETTER ***
270 GOTO 140
280 REM *** ERROR! ***
290 POKE 53280,2
300 FOR DE = 1 TO 20:NEXT DE
310 POKE 53280,254
320 GOTO 200
```

29.

Home Inventory Log

A home inventory log is a good idea. Should the misfortune of burglary, hurricane, or fire ever befall you, it becomes much easier for the police department to reunite you with your possessions, or for an insurance company to accurately process your claim. But what if you use a computer to record model numbers and serial numbers and the diskette burns up in the fire? Do you have a fireproof safe in the study? It may not help.

Cassette and diskette files may melt. So it's a good idea to back up that information on paper as well. Printer paper has a flash point of about 1400 degrees and will survive long after a tape has melted into a big lump of goo. It would be even better to store your log in an inexpensive safety deposit box where you bank.

To use the program, type the number 1, 2, or 3. The number 1 will call up the part of the program that will allow logging each possession, item by item. Fill in a descriptive name, the purchase price, and serial number.

When you're done, hit just the return key when it asks for the item's name. That closes the file you've just writ-ten and sends you back to the menu. Type the number 2, and you can read the inventory log. If you've made some new purchases and want to add them to the list, type in number 1, and the information will be added to the bottom of a new file. If you've finished working with the program, a 3 will end it.

How the Program Works

Line 180 dimensions the variables we'll be using to send information from the keyboard to the inventory log.

Lines 220 through 310 format and display the task menu.

Line 320 gets the user's choice, and line 340 sends the program off to do its work.

Line 380 asks for the name of this inventory log and opens it.

Line 400 blanks the screen.

Line 410 displays the header, or title page, if you will.

Line 430 asks for the name of the item to be recorded.

Line 460 watches for the user to enter a carriage return as the only response to an item request. This done, the file is closed and control loops back to the task menu.

Lines 470 through 500 input the serial number and price information.

Lines 520 through 550 write the item, its price, and serial number to the inventory file.

126

Lines 630 through 650 ask for the name of the file to be read. By the way, it doesn't have to be an inventory file. You can just as easily read a letter you've written.

Lines 690 through 730 read and display twenty lines at a time.

Line 730 waits for any key to be pressed before allowing a read of another twenty lines. This is a big help when there's a lot of information to plow through. Without this subroutine, the text would flash past faster than even a speed reader could absorb.

Line 740 watches for when the program reads to the bottom of a file. When it does, line 760 will close the file.

Lines 820 through 840 display the goodbye message and end the program.

String and Numeric Variables

KE$(KE) Tells which job you want done.

FI$ The name of the file to be opened.

IT$ Name of the item being recorded.

PR$ Price paid for item.

SE$ Serial number of item being recorded.

CO Number of lines read and displayed.

```
100 REM *************************
110 REM *
120 REM *
130 REM *** HOME INVENTORY LOG ***
140 REM *
150 REM *
160 REM *************************
170 REM *** DIMENSION VARIABLES ***
180 DIM FI$(20),IT$(79),PR$(79),SES(39)
190 PRINT CHR$(147)
200 REM *** DISPLAY TASK MENU ***
210 REM *** BLACK LETTERS ***
220 PRINT CHR$(144)
230 PRINT SPC(2) "HOME INVENTORY LOG"
240 PRINT
250 REM *** WHITE LETTERS ***
260 PRINT CHR$(5)
270 PRINT "1. LOG POSSESSIONS"
280 PRINT
290 PRINT "2. READ INVENTORY"
300 PRINT
310 PRINT "3. QUIT ";
320 GET KE$: IF KE$ = "" THEN 720
330 KE = ASC(VE$)
340 ON KE - 48 GOTO 360,620,820
350 GOTO 190
360 PRINT CHR$(147)
370 PRINT SPC(2) "RECORD POSSESSIONS"
380 PRINT:PRINT "FILE SAVED AS ";:INPUT FI$
390 OPEN 1,1,2,FI$
400 PRINT CHR$(147)
410 PRINT SPC(3) "HOME INVENTORY"
420 PRINT
430 PRINT "ITEM ";:INPUT 1T$
440 PRINT
450 REM *** RETURN WHEN DONE ***
460 IF 1T$ = "" THEN CLOSE 1: GOTO 190
470 PRINT:PRINT "PURCHASE PRICE"
```

128

```
480 INPUT PR$
490 PRINT:PRINT "SERIAL NUMBER"
500 INPUT SE$
510 REM *** RECORD INFORMATION ***
520 PRINT#1,IT$
530 PRINT#1,PR$
540 PRINT#1,SE$
550 PRINT#1,CHR$(141)
560 REM *** NEXT ENTRY ***
570 1T$ = "" 580 GOTO 420
590 REM *********************
600 REM *** READ INVENTORY ***
610 REM *********************
620 PRINT CHR$(147)
630 PRINT SPC(4)"READ INVENTORY"
640 PRINT
650 PRINT"FILE SAVED AS ";;INPUT FI$
660 OPEN 1,1,0,FIS
670 PRINT CHR$(147)
680 REM *** READ 1ST LINE FROM FILE ***
690 INPUT#1,TT$
700 REM *** COUNT LINES DISPLAYED ***
710 CO = CO + 1
720 PRINT ITS
730 IF CO >20 THEN GET KE$:IF KE$ = "" THEN 770:CO = 0
740 IF ST x 64 THEN 690
750 REM *** CLOSE WHEN DONE READING *
760 CLOSE 1
770 GET KE$:IF KE$ = "" THEN 770
780 GOTO 190
790 REM *******************
800 REM *** QUIT ROUTINE ***
810 REM *******************
820 PRINT
830 PRINT SPC(9) "BYE'"
840 END
```

30.

Tax Deduction Recorder

Organization yields better results in almost any venture. And when the final consideration is whether or not you'll be able to declare all your justified deductions, that method of organization be comes an important aspect of tax records. This system is simple. Once every day, week, or month—or at the conclusion of a business trip—sit down with all your receipts. Sort them in chronological order; then enter each one. Log each kind of deduction—entertainment, travel, meals, whatever. Also record the item purchased—lunch, newspaper, or financial report. Next enter the dollar amount, followed by the date. With the receipts gathered into this expense ledger, yearly tax calculations will be smoother, and much less suspect if ever con-tested by the IRS.

How the Program Works

Line 180 dimensions and declares the string variables. Line 190 blanks the screen. Lines 220 through 310 format and display the task menu.

Line 320 gets the user's choice of tasks, and line 340 sends the pro-gram off to perform that task. If the user entered any number other than a 1,2, or 3, then line 350 sends the pro-gram back to line 190 to ask for the menu selection all over again.

Lines 360 through 440 display the prompt asking for the tax file- name. There are a number of ways to organize such a set of files. If more than one person is using the computer, assign different filenames, such as: JOHN. TAX, or ETHEL. TAX. Another option is to use the extender as a calendar flag, such as JOHN .FEB, and JOHN.MAR. or, just hit RETURN if you don't want to be bothered.

Lines 400 and 410 blank the screen and print the title page, also known as the header.

Lines 430 through 480 input the deduction, along with all pertinent Information relating to category, and so on.

Lines 520 through 550 write this information to the appropriate file.

Line 460 meanwhile has been watching for a carriage return. After the program asks for a deduction, if you hit return, and nothing else, that signals the program you are done. Then, line 460 will close the file, and send us back to the task menu.

Lines 620 through 650 will ask for the tax file you wish to review and then open it for a read.

Line 740 sets the trap that will look for the end of the file. When it's encountered, the pro- gram lumbers off to line 770, waiting for you to hit any key before displaying the task menu.

Lines 690 through 730 read twenty lines of deductions at a time. Hit any key to see the next twenty, and so on.

Lines 820 through 840 close the file and return us to the menu.

String and Numeric Variables

AM$ Amount paid.

DE $ Category of deduction.

DA$ Date when expense occurred.

FI$ Filename where information will be stored.

KE$(KE) Do which job in menu?

CO Number of lines read and displayed from tax file.

ST Status of cassette recorder.

```
100 REM ***********************************
110 REM *
120 REM *
130 REM *** INCOME TAX DEDUCTION RECORDER ***
140 REM *
150 REM *
160 REM ***********************************
170 REM *** DIMENSION VARIABLES ***
180 DIM DE$(35),DA$(10),AM$(19),FI$(12)
190 PRINT CHR$(147)
200 REM *** DISPLAY TASK MENU ***
210 REM *** BLACK LETTERS ***
220 PRINT CHR$(144)
230 PRINT SPC(4) "TAX PACKAGE"
240 PRINT
250 REM *** WHITE LETTERS ***
260 PRINT CHR$(5)
270 PRINT "1. RECORD DEDUCTIONS"
280 PRINT
290 PRINT "2. SEE DEDUCTIONS"
300 PRINT
310 PRINT "3. QUIT ";
320 GET KE$: IF KE$ = "" THEN 720
330 KE = ASC(VE$)
740 ON KE - 48 GOTO 360,620,820
350 GOTO 190
360 PRINT CHR$(147)
370 PRINT SPC(2) "RECORD DEDUCTIONS"
380 PRINT:PRINT "FILE SAVED AS ";:INPUT F1$
390 OPEN 1,1,1,F1$
400 PRINT CHR$(147)
410 PRINT SPC(7) "TAX DEDUCTIONS"
420 PRINT
430 PRINT:INPUT "DEDUCTION"; DE$
440 PRINT
450 REM *** RETURN WHEN DONE ***
460 IF DE$ = "" THEN CLOSE 1: GOTO 190
470 PRINT:INPUT "DATE";DA$
```

```
480 PRINT:INPUT "AMOUNT";AM$
490 REM *************************
500 REM *** RECORD INFORMATION ***
510 REM *************************
520 PRINT#1,DE$
530 PR1NT#1,DA$
540 PRINT#1,AM$
550 PRINT#1,CHR$(141)
560 REM *** NEXT ENTRY ***
570 DE$ = ""
580 GOTO 420
590 REM **********************
600 REM *** READ TAX FILE ***
610 REM **********************
620 PRINT CHR$(147)
630 PRINT SPC(4)"READ TAX FILES"
640 PRINT
650 PRINT"FILE SAVED AS ";:INPUT F1$
660 OPEN 1,1,0,F1$
670 PRINT CHR$(147)
680 REM *** READ 1ST LINE FROM FILE ***
690 INPUT#1,DE$
700 REM *** COUNT LINES DISPLAYED ***
710 CO = CO + 1
720 PRINT DE$
730 IF CO =20 THEN GET KE$:IF KE$ = "" THEN 730:CO =0
740 IF ST <> 64 THEN 690
750 REM *** CLOSE WHEN DONE READING *
760 CLOSE 1
770 GET KE$ :IF KE$ = "" THEN 770
780 GOTO 190
790 REM *******************
800 REM *** QUIT ROUTINE ***
810 REM *******************
820 PRINT
830 PRINT SPC(9) "BYE'"
840 END
```

31

Jogger's Electronic Logbook

Are you an aficionado of runner's high? Perhaps you've read the earlier chapter on weight control and have chosen running as a method for achieving and maintaining physical and mental well being. Regardless of the motivation, sometimes it's nice to know where you've been. Are your times getting faster? Are you feeling stronger? How does your conditioning compare to what it was a year ago? The jog book will save your sport's vital statistics for later comparison. As it's set up, you can enter a day's run or view the whole logbook. In recording the day's run, you may prefer to jot down elapsed times and type them into the computer in one sitting every couple of days or once a week.

In the body of the program, you will be asked for how far you ran, how long it took, and how you felt afterwards. On a scale of one to ten, with ten measuring euphoria, how did you feel? Here's where there's room for modification. How did you feel before you ran? How did you feel after you ran? Which matters most to you? There's room to enter both; just separate them by a few spaces.

If you'd like to recount your exercise sessions, type in the number 3 at the menu, and the results of your miles and miles of aerobic activity will display on the screen one day at a time. Hit any key to see the next day's run. When finished either entering a run or perusing the log, the program will jump back to the menu. Typing a number 4 at the menu will end the program.

How the Program Works

Line 170 declares and dimensions the string variables.

Lines 210 through 320 format and display the menu.

Line 330 waits for you to hit a key.

When you do, line 350 checks to see if you typed a "4", meaning you want to quit.

Lines 390 through 490 ask which file you want to work with. One way to organize your logs would be to break them down into calendar months. For instance, when asked, type the runner's name followed by a month's abbreviation. When you do, line 460 will concatenate, or join them together into one name.

Lines 530 through 550 create a file the first time you write to it.

Lines 590 through 980 update a file as you log a new running day's statistics. In more detail, line 590 creates a temporary file where we'll store the figures of one or more days. Later on, we'll add these figures to the existing file.

Lines 630 through 720 ask for the pertinent information, such as how far you ran and how long it took. If you hit a RETURN when the program asks you for the day's date, line 660 stops with the questions and closes the file.

Lines 730 through 760 write all the miles and elapsed times to the temporary file named: ADD.SEQ.

Line 860 opens the command channel to the disk drive that allows us to merge the new file with the old. Line 880 makes copy of the existing runner's log, naming it "LOG".

Line 900 merges the file we just wrote, named: "ADD", with the copy of the original named: "LOG". The result is named: "UPDATE".

Line 920 erases the original file; while line 940 renames UPDATE with whatever the original and now deceased file used to be called.

Line 960 erases all of the temporary files.

Line 970 closes the command channel.

Lines 1020 through 1200 read the jogger's log.

Line 1020 opens the file; while lines 1030 through 1060 read the first four items stored there.

Lines 1070 through 1140 display the information.

Line 1150 checks the file to see whether or not we've read to the end.

If so, then CLOSE the file in line 1180. If not, wait for any key to be pressed before reading the next day's re corded run.

Lines 1240 through 1260 display the finished message and end the program.

String and Numeric Variables

KES(KE) Any key pressed.
NA$ Runner's name. MO$ Month to be logged.
DA$ Date of run.
MI$ Miles run.
ET$ Elapsed time.
EN$ Runner's mood, before, after, or both.

The Program

```
100 REM ********************************
110 REM *
120 REM *
130 REM *** JOGGER'S ELECTRONIC LOGBOOK ***
140 REM *
150 REM *
160 REM ********************************
170 DIM NA$(22),MO$(12),DA$(20),MI$(4),ET$(8),EN$(4)
180 REM *******************
190 REM *** DISPLAY MENU ***
200 REM *******************
210 PRINT CHR$(147)
220 PRINT SPC(5) "JOGGER LOG"
230 PRINT:PRINT
240 PRINT"1. START LOG"
250 PRINT
260 PRINT"2. UPDATE LOG"
270 PRINT
280 PRINT"3. READ LOG"
290 PRINT
300 PRINT"4. DONE"
310 PRINT:PRINT
320 PRINT "SELECT 1 - 4 ";
330 GET KE$: IF KE$ = "" THEN 330
340 KE = ASC(KES)
350 IF KE > 51 THEN 1240
360 REM *******************
370 REM *** CHOOSE A FILE ***
380 REM *******************
390 PRINT CHR$(147)
400 PRINT SPC(5) "WHICH FILE"
410 PRINT:PRINT
420 INPUT "RUNNER";NA$
430 PRINT:PRINT
440 INPUT "MONTH"; MO$
450 PRINT:PRINT
```

```
460 NA$ = NA$ + MO$
470 PRINT NA$
480 PRINT CHR$(147)
490 ON KE - 48 GOTO 530,590,1020
500 REM ******************
510 REM *** CREATE FILE ***
520 REM ******************
530 PRINT:PRINT
540 OPEN 1,8,2,NA$ + ",SEQ,W"
550 CLOSE 1
560 REM ****************************
570 REM *** CREATE TEMPORARY FILE ***
580 REM ****************************
590 OPEN 1,8,2,"@0:ADD,SEQ,W"
600 REM *****:*************
610 REM *** UPDATE LOG ***
620 REM *****************
630 PRINT SPC(4) "RECORD THE RUN"
640 PRINT:PRINT
650 INPUT "DATE";DA$
660 IF DA$ = "" THEN 800
670 PRINT:PRINT
680 INPUT "MILES RUN";MI$
690 PRINT:PRINT
700 INPUT "ELAPSED TIME";ET$
710 PRINT:PRINT
720 INPUT "ENERGY LEVEL";EN$
730 PRINT#1,DA$
740 PRINT#1,MI$
750 PRINT#1,ET$
760 PRINT#1,EN$
770 DA$ = ""
780 PRINT CHR$(147)
790 GOTO 650
800 CLOSE 1
810 REM ***********************
820 REM *** DISK FILE CLEAN-UP ***
830 REM ***********************
840 PRINT CHR$(147)
850 PRINT "PLEASE WAIT .
```

```
860 OPEN 15,8,15
870 REM *** DUPLICATE ORIGINAL FILE ***
880 PRINT#15,"COPY@0:LOG="+ NA$
890 REM *** MERGE DUPLICATE WITH TEMPORARY ***
900 PRINT#15,"COPY@0:UPDATE=LOG,ADD"
910 REM *** ERASE ORIGINAL ***
920 PRINT#15,"S:"+NA$
930 REM *** RENAME MERGED FILES AS ORIGINAL ***
940 PRINT#15,"RENAME@0:" + NA$ + "=UPDATE"
950 REM *** ERASE TEMPORARY FILES ***
960 PRINT#15,"S:ADD,LOG,UPDATE"
970 CLOSE 15
980 GOTO 210
990 REM ***************************
1000 REM *** BROWSE THROUGH FILE ***
1010 REM ***************************
1020 OPEN 1,8,2,NA$
1030 INPUT#1,DA$
1040 INPUT#1,MI$
1050 INPUT#1,ET$
1060 INPUT#1,EN$
1070 PRINT "DATE ";DA$ 1080 PRINT
1090 PRINT "MILES RUN ";MI$
1100 PRINT
1110 PRINT "ELAPSED TIME ";ET$
1120 PRINT
1130 PRINT "ENERGY LEVEL ";EN$
1140 PRINT:PRINT
1150 IF ST <> 0 THEN 1180
1160 GET KE$: IF KE$ = "" THEN 1160
1170 GOTO 1030
1180 CLOSE 1
1190 GET KE$: IF KE$ = "" THEN 1190
1200 GOTO 210
1210 REM ****************************
1220 REM *** FINISHED, END PROGRAM ***
1230 REM ****************************
1240 PRINT:PRINT
1250 PRINT "DON'T FORGET TO RUN TOMORROW!"
1260 END
```

32.

Credit Card Manager

Do you like to keep track of purchases made with your credit card? It's easy with this diskette file manager. RUN the program and choose between RECORDing a purchase, READing the file, or QUIT-ting.

Just enter a number 1, 2, or 3. No return is necessary. For the moment, let's assume you chose Record a Purchase, by typing the number 1.

The screen will blank for a moment then ask the name under which you are storing the credit card purchase information.

If you don't want a filename, simply hit the RETURN key. Next, a prompt will ask for the name of the item bought, how much was paid for it, and the date of the purchase. Is there more than one item to record? If so, keep plugging in the information.

When you'd like to quit, at the NAME OF ITEM prompt, hit RETURN and no other key. Control will loop back to the task menu. This time choose the number 2 and enter the file where the credit card information is stored. Twenty lines at a time will be read from the file and displayed on the TV screen.

Hit any key to scroll another twenty lines of financial facts. When the file is empty, a message will inform you. Again, hit any key, but this time, instead of more dollars-and-cents figures, you'll see the task menu. If finished with all this financial wizardry, type the number 3 and the program will end.

How the Program Works

Line 180 dimensions the string variables.
Line 190 blanks the screen.
Lines 220 through 310 display and format the task menu.
Line 340 sends the program off to perform its assigned task. If the choice was

anything other than the numbers 1 through 3, the program demands a menu selection all over again.

Lines 360 through 380 ask for the filename to be written to.

Line 400 opens the filename.

Lines 420 through 450 ask for the credit card information and write it to the file. Here's more detail: A prompt appears on the screen asking for the name of the item, the amount paid, and the date of purchase.

Line 470, by the way, looks for a carriage return. Hit the RETURN key when you're through entering.

Lines 530 through 560 write all the information to the file.

Lines 630 through 660 ask for the credit card file you would like to review.

Line 670 opens that file.

Lines 700 through 740 read and print the credit card file, or any other file, twenty lines at a time.

Lines 750 through 780 watch for the end of file, close it, and wait for any key to be pressed before sending us back to the task menu.

Lines 830 through 850 are the quit routine and end the program.

String and Numeric Variables

AM$ Cost of purchase.

IT$ Name of item bought. DA$ When the purchase was made.

FI$ Name of the file we will read or write to.

CO Controls reading and printing twenty lines at a time from the file. KE$(KE) Any key pressed yet?

The Program

```
100 REM **********************
110 REM *
120 REM *
130 REM * CREDIT CARD MANAGER *
140 REM *
150 REM *
160 REM **********************
170 REM *** DIMENSION VARIABLES ***
180 DIM AM$(35),DA$(10),IT$(29),FI$(12)
190 PRINT CHR$(147)
200 REM *** DISPLAY TASK MENU ***
210 REM *** BLACK LETTERS ***
220 PRINT CHR$(144)
230 PRINT SPC(2) "CREDIT CARD MANAGER"
240 PRINT 250 REM *** WHITE LETTERS ***
260 PRINT CHR$(5)
270 PRINT "1. RECORD PURCHASE"
280 PRINT
290 PRINT "2. READ FILE"
300 PRINT
310 PRINT "3. QUIT ";
320 GET KES: IF KES = "" THEN 320
330 KE = ASC(KE$)
340 ON KE - 48 GOTO 360,630,830
350 GOTO 190
360 PRINT CHR$(147)
370 PRINT SPC(2) "RECORD PURCHASE"
380 PRINT:PRINT "FILE SAVED AS ";:INPUT FIS
390 REM *** OPEN CASSETTE FILE FOR WRITE ***
400 OPEN 1,1,1,FI$
410 PRINT CHR$(147) 420 PRINT SPC(3) "RECORD INFO"
430 PRINT
440 PRINT:INPUT "PURCHASED";IT$
450 PRINT
460 REM *** RETURN WHEN DONE ***
470 IF IT$ = "" THEN CLOSE 1: GOTO 190
480 PRINT:INPUT "DATE";DA$
490 PRINT:INPUT "AMOUNT";AM$
```

142

```
500 REM **************************
510 REM *** RECORD INFORMATION ***
520 REM **************************
530 PRINT#1,IT$
540 PRINT#1,DA$
550 PRINT#1,AM$
560 PRINT#1,CHR$(141)
570 REM *** NEXT ENTRY ***
580 ITS = ""
590 GOTO 430
600 REM *********************
610 REM *** READ PURCHASES ***
620 REM *********************
630 PRINT CHR$(147)
640 PRINT "READ CREDIT CARD FILES"
650 PRINT
660 PRINT"FILE SAVED AS ";:INPUT FIS
670 OPEN 1,1,0,FIS
680 PRINT CHR$(147)
690 REM *** READ 1ST LINE FROM FILE ***
700 INPUT#1,DE$
710 REM *** COUNT LINES DISPLAYED ***
720 CO = CO + 1
730 PRINT DE$
740 IF CO >20 THEN GET KE$:IF KE$ = "" THEN 740:CO = 0
750 IF ST <> 64 THEN 700
760 REM *** CLOSE WHEN DONE READING ***
770 CLOSE 1
780 GET KE$: IF KE$ = "" THEN 780
790 GOTO 190
800 REM ********************
810 REM *** QUIT ROUTINE ***
820 REM ********************
830 PRINT
840 PRINT SPC(9) "BYE!"
850 END
```

Made in the USA
Las Vegas, NV
02 February 2022

42901320R00089